Heal Yourself to Happiness

A Simple Guide to Raising Your
Vibrations and Achieving the
Health, Prosperity and Love
You Desire

Deborah Jane Sutton

Cover Design by Ida Sveningsson at
www.idafiasveningsson.se

Edited by Laura Barnes at
www.palavermaven.co.uk

Formatted by Angie Mroczka at
www.authorgeek.com

ISBN: 978-1522890782

I dedicate this book to you, the reader. I hope it may touch your heart in the same way it has touched mine to write. Remember you are essentially pure love and I send you more love and light on your journey as you Raise your Vibrations and Heal Yourself to greater Happiness.

Disclaimer

I would like to point out that I am sharing information and opinions in this book. I am not an expert in the medical field and I trust that you will exercise your own common sense and take responsibility for your own health and actions.

Contents

Introduction

I have been prompted to write this book because every day I meet so many people, and not just clients, who are not happy with their lives in one way or another. They are dissatisfied with their health, their bodies, their lack of money, their single status and, most of all, their jobs.

I want to tell them, show them, just how easy it is to achieve whatever it is they want in this life. I want to explain to them the basic concepts behind manifesting their dreams and desires. I do remember, however, when I was in their shoes; when I didn't realise how these things worked; when I didn't understand the concept of the "Law of Attraction" and "Thought Energy" and how we can use it to create our own reality. I didn't understand the importance of literally raising our vibrations. That's why I've made this book easy to read and simple—with practical steps that can be easily applied to your life to help you do just that—Raise Your Vibrations—and in so doing, change whole areas of your life.

My career has led me to this point of teaching others how to create the health, love and happiness they desire and deserve where peace and prosperity are welcomed side effects. For many years I was a school teacher and studied Reflexology, Reiki and other Holistic Therapies as a hobby. I began to understand the importance of releasing stress and trapped emotions from our bodies. I could see from my own life and those around me, how negative emotional experiences affected our health and not just in the short term. I could see how characters and personalities were formed and moulded with every emotional trauma. I could almost feel the presence of trapped negative emotions within my own body. It became clear to me that I had to explore ways in which to release these emotions and not just for myself. I could see the need for this release in others. This led me to study Emotional Freedom Technique, The Emotion Code and The Body Code (by Dr Bradley Nelson) which in turn led me to explore the role our "minds" play in our health and happiness and so I studied PSYCH K® and other aspects of Energy Psychology.

I am my own best advert. Since applying the simple steps I have outlined here in this book, I have found inner joy and peace, lost over 20 kilos (3st or 44lbs), met and married my Mr Right, not seen a doctor for over 5 years and left the 'day job' in order to follow my heart. I am now healthier and happier than I have ever been and *YOU* can be too!

Why wait? Start today—start NOW! When it comes to our health we don't have time to waste. Read just how simple it is to Heal Yourself to Happiness.

"Your body's ability to heal is greater than anyone has ever permitted you to believe"
—Anon

Chapter 1:
Affirmations

What Are Affirmations and Why Are They Important?

I can't start a book on Self Healing without mentioning the importance of affirmations. For me and many others starting out on this path of self discovery and greater health and happiness, affirmations really *are* the first step. But what exactly *are* affirmations?

To affirm means to say something positively. It means to declare firmly and assert something to be true. Affirmations are statements where you assert that what you want to be true *is* true. They are basically just positive statements. Short, powerful statements. Yet their impact is profound. Affirmations are you being in conscious control of your thoughts. When you say them or think them or even hear them, they become the thoughts that create your reality. Affirmations, therefore, are your conscious thoughts.

Some researchers have recorded that we have between 45,000 and 51,000 thoughts a day. Others claim it's more like 70,000. Personally, I don't know how many thoughts we have per day and I'm sure some people have more thoughts than others but what I am sure about is that most of the thoughts that run through our minds on a daily basis are subconscious and negative in nature. Especially that ongoing, running commentary that we give ourselves.

Our subconscious makes up about 90% of our mind whereas our conscious mind makes up only about 10%. Therefore, our subconscious mind is so much more powerful than our conscious mind. How many times do you berate yourself and beat yourself up in your head about the way you have dealt with a situation? Or about the way you said something to someone? Or about what you're eating? or doing? or think you *should* be doing? The point is that repeating Affirmations make you consciously aware of your thoughts. When you start making conscious, positive thoughts, you actually become more aware of the negative thoughts that are always threatening to take over and you can start to train the subconscious mind to accept the new, positive thought.

"I am worthy of great health and happiness"

We can't discuss the use of affirmations without first acknowledging and appreciating the lovely Louise Hay who is undoubtedly the Queen of Affirmations. Her book, *You Can Heal Your Life*, was the beginning of my conscious journey to inner love, acceptance and greater joy. This, by its pure nature, led to my improved health, abundance, vision and happiness. For this reason, not only am I a big fan of affirmations, but I also love helping others understand How and Why they are so important to Self Healing and Happiness.

Clients often complain that they don't feel comfortable with saying affirmations because they feel empty or the sentences get stuck in their throats for the simple reason that they perceive them as "lies".

Let's take the example,

"I love myself so I lovingly feed myself nourishing foods and beverages."

If you haven't learned to fully love yourself yet this one might get stuck and indeed it may just bring to your mind the fact (and guilt and shame) that you regularly eat junk food and drink fizzy drinks. If this is your reflex response thought to this affirmation then you can either focus on the love you *do* have for yourself and the aspects of your diet that *are* nourishing. Even if this is small, at least it's *true*. By repeating the affirmation morning, noon and night you will find that you will slowly love yourself more each day and slowly increase the amount of your diet that *is* nourishing.

If this still does not resonate with you and it just makes you feel worse (we can't have that) then you can *downsize* the affirmation.

For example, by using the words " I am changing" or "I am willing"

"I am changing the way I think about food."

"I am willing to love and accept myself."

"I am willing to improve my diet."

"I am willing to feed my body nourishing foods and beverages"

But you do have to do it. Believe me it works.

We can do the same for other affirmations too, for example, abundance affirmations. When trying to manifest more money into their lives many people get stuck because they focus on what they *don't have* rather than what they do *have*. If you focus on *"lack"* then the Universe will give you *more "lack"*. Everything is energy. We emit a vibrational frequency and by the pure nature of Science (yes, Science) the Universe will bring back to us that same frequency. So when you emit the frequency of lack, you will receive more lack. Whereas, if you emit the frequency of gratitude, the Universe will bring you *more* things to be grateful for. If you emit *love*, it will send you *more love*. It's *so* simple! Some people refer to it as "The Secret" (Rhonda Byrne's famous book and film) but I prefer the word "Concept" because, to me, it's such a logical concept.

So as you focus every morning, noon and night on the nourishing aspects of your diet, the good things about your body, the things you *do* have and *are* grateful for and the abundance you actually *already* have, the Universe will match it and bring you *more*. Now that's ABUNDANCE!

Boosting the Power of Your Affirmations

To boost the power of your affirmations you need to raise your vibrations so try visualising your desired result as you say your affirmations. Visualise the body you want to have for example. Make sure it's *your* body you visualise and not anyone else's. You have no idea what's inside other people's bodies. As they say, be careful what you wish for. Visualise your bills paid, visualise driving the car you want, visualise a soul mate, visualise the activity you want to be doing .... I mean *really* imagine you already have it. *See* it. What does it look like? *Smell* it. What does it smell like? *Hear* and *Taste* it. *Feel* it. What does it feel like? *Sense* the whole thing. Now *this* will raise your vibrations to receiving whatever it may be. If a negative or contradictory thought enters your head, just let it go, and keep going.

Some people find affirmations are more powerful and effective said while doing their favourite pastime such as, yoga, for example, at a time when their vibrations are already high. Personally, I find repeating them while swimming is powerful but then you have to find *your* thing. The Thing that makes your Heart Sing and say them then.

I had no idea how powerful affirmations could be. I just repeated this first set of affirmations from Louise Hay's book and said them without knowing or believing any of this. I had typed them up and printed them off. I had a copy by my bed which I said every morning and every night. I had a smaller copy of them folded up in my pencil case at work. I would take them out whenever I had a spare moment and read through them. After a while I found it really comforting to do so. Then, just seeing the folded paper in my pencil case would trigger the thoughts of these affirmations. After all, it is the thoughts behind affirmations that create the real healing.

It was only later on, one day while saying them to myself as I always did while swimming up and down in the pool, that I realised all my affirmations had come true! Honestly. I realised that I *had* and I *was* everything that I was saying. It was an amazing and exciting realisation for me. Whether it was physical manifestations or my perception of things that had changed is an interesting point to explore but my affirmations had *all* become, indeed, *true* for me.

"Deep in the centre of my being is an infinite well of Love. I now allow this Love to flow to the surface. It fills my heart, my body, my mind, my consciousness, my very being, and radiates out from me in all directions and returns to me multiplied. The more Love I use and give, the more I have to give, the supply is endless. The use of Love makes me feel good. It is an expression of my inner joy.

I Love myself therefore I take Loving care of my body. I Lovingly feed it nourishing foods and beverages.

I lovingly groom it and dress it and my body Lovingly responds to me with vibrant health and energy.

I Love myself therefore I provide for myself a comfortable home, one that fills all my needs and is a pleasure to be in. I fill the rooms with the vibration of Love so that all who enter, myself included, will feel this Love and be nourished by it.

I Love myself therefore I work at a job that I truly enjoy doing, one that uses my creative talents and abilities working with and for people that I Love and that Love me, and earning a good income.

I Love myself, therefore, I behave and think in a Loving way to all people for I know that that which I give out returns to me multiplied. I only attract Loving people in my world for they are a mirror of what I am.

I Love myself, therefore, I forgive and totally release the past and all past experiences and I am free.

I Love myself, therefore, I live totally in the now, experiencing each moment as good and knowing that my future is bright and joyous, and secure for I am a beloved child of the universe and the universe Lovingly takes care of me now and forever more. And so it is."

—Louise Hay, "You Can Heal Your Life" (1984) Hay House, Inc., Carlsbad, CA (Reproduced with kind permission from Hay House.)

I quickly wrote out 8 more affirmations to fit my new desires. I took these from Louise Hay's film *"You Can Heal Your Life"* because they were all encompassing and relevant to me (to everyone I don't doubt). These, too, soon became my reality.

All my relationships are harmonious

I am deeply fulfilled by all that I do

Every experience is a success

I deserve the best and I accept it now

I lovingly listen to my body's messages

I am happy, healthy, whole, complete and secure

I express gratitude for all that is good in my life

Each day brings wonderful new surprises

Another way to boost the impact of your affirmations is to make them rhyme. This will help them stick in your head more and, like an advertisement's jingle or pop song, they will more easily repeat in your head and hopefully get stuck.

I also recommend helping your affirmations come to fruition by writing them down on pieces of paper and sticking them around your rooms. Every time you see the paper they are written on your subconscious mind will think of the affirmation.

In my days as a primary school teacher I used to get the kids to enjoy Brain Gym exercises before class. We all have a creative side and a logical side to our brains and some people are really dominant in the use of one or other of these sides. Brain Gym activities help us balance both sides of the brain and I have seen the benefits of this in the classroom. The idea is that the predominantly logical thinkers can increase their creativity before a literacy lesson and the predominantly creative thinkers can increase their powers of logic before a maths class. Either way, integrating both sides of our brain allows us to accept new information more readily. Simple Brain Gym exercises include standing up, lifting up your right knee and touching it with your left elbow followed by raising your left knee and touching it with your right elbow. Repeating this action while saying your affirmations would help boost their power and it would certainly make them more fun!

I have said repeat them morning, noon and night but to really boost their power, say them much *more* than that! When you first wake up, while cleaning your teeth, while in the shower, while doing your hair, while driving to work, if you're busy all day at work, say them when you go to the toilet. Just keep repeating them. Try and say them with total *belief*. Even if none of this is resonating with you and you still don't believe they can work *still* just *say* them. Remember, you want your conscious thoughts to outnumber those pesky negative subconscious thoughts so the more you say them the better. You are, in effect, retraining your subconscious mind.

Remember, don't focus on *how* your affirmations will come to fruition. Just trust that they will. The Universe will do the rest.

Wording Your Affirmations

Affirmations always need to be in the present tense. If you say, for example, " I will have a beautiful body", "I will have an increased income" then the Universe will match that vibration of *not* having it *now*. So keep your affirmations in the present. Also, keep them more general in nature. The word Abundance is great. It covers so much. It covers everything!

Try not to be too specific. If you're wanting to meet Mr or Mrs Right then use these terms. Don't mention a person you fancy by name. The Universe probably has someone better in mind for you anyway. If you want a new car, refer to it as "the perfect car for me" and not to mention the exact make, model etc The Universe will know better than you as to which car is the perfect one for you. You don't want to hinder the manifestation.

"The perfect car for me is making its way to me now"

Remember to visualise driving it, smell it, feel it and hear it. This will raise your vibrations to match actually receiving it.

Focus on what it is you want rather than what you don't want. Don't use negatives in your affirmations. For example, the statement "*I don't have debts*" will not work because it gives its attention to the idea of debt and guess what? yes, the Universe will match it with more debt. If you say "*I have more money* ", this is better but you are still focussing on the idea that you don't have much *now* or not as much as you want. There is still a sense of *lack*. Compare it to,

"I welcome money into my life."

"I am prosperous."

"I welcome prosperity into my life."

"I welcome Abundance."

You can progress to "I can easily pay my bills."

"I am a magnet for money." etc

Choosing Your Affirmations

So here's the Exercise. I have a long list of affirmations here and I want you to slowly read them and acknowledge your *first* thought response to each one. If you can read it comfortably then there's a chance you believe it and you can move on. If your mind jumps to one or two things that contradict the statement then you could be nearly there but with some issues to clear up making that particular affirmation a good option for you to adopt.

Now if you repeat one and it gets really stuck in your throat, then that's the one (or ones) you need to focus on the most. Or if reading them makes you cringe, cry or want to laugh, they are the ones you need. If they don't resonate with you, then why not? Do you want them to be true? If so, write it down and start saying it. Morning, noon and night.

I love and accept myself unconditionally

I radiate love and respect and in return I get love and respect

I am free to make my own choices and decisions

I accept compliments easily and freely compliment others

I accept others as they are and they in turn accept me as I am

I deserve all that is good and I accept it now.

The universe supports me.

My mind is filled with loving, healthy, positive and prosperous thoughts which ultimately become my reality.

My mind is full of gratitude for my wonderful life and everything in it.

I release the past and live only in the present.

I am free to be happy and healthy

My body heals itself naturally and quickly

My mind, body and spirit are harmoniously balanced

I lovingly nourish my physical body

I see beauty in all parts of my body

I love and accept my body as it is and as it changes

I now allow the healing energy of love to flow through me

I welcome prosperity into my life

Money is a wonderful tool that I use to create possibilities for me and for others

The universe is a friendly place and willingly gives me everything I need

I deserve to have all the money I need

It is ok to have more money than I need

I receive and accept money with love and gratitude

I allow myself to earn good money

I prosper wherever I turn

I am ready, willing and able to be the best me that I can be

I allow my visions and dreams to become reality

I have the ability to create my life as I want it to be

It is easy for me to give love to others

It is easy for me to receive love from others

I am worthy of having an intimate and passionate relationship

For those of you who can Self Muscle Test, repeat each statement and muscle test yourself. A positive response indicates that your subconscious mind already believes the statement. You can muscle test on each statement until you find one that tests negative. That's the one to work on. In Chapter 4, I explain the importance of Muscle Testing and how you can do it. However, for the purpose of this exercise you can test how your inner self feels about each affirmation by just calming your mind and your breathing and listening to your initial response as you say each one. Your body will tell you if you truly believe it or not. Which ones would you like to be true?

Here are some more favourites of mine that I regularly say together

Everything I need to know is revealed to me

Everything I need comes to me in the perfect time space sequence

Life is a Joy and full of Love

I am healthy and full of energy

I am loving, lovable and loved

I prosper wherever I turn

I am changing and growing

I am grateful for all that is good in my life

I am an unlimited being, receiving unlimited abundance from an unlimited Source in unlimited ways.

Now, which ones didn't feel right for you? Which ones got stuck in your throat? Or made you cringe? Which ones tested negative when muscle testing? Make a short list, about 8 is good, and say them. Morning, noon and night.

"I am willing to change"

"I am learning to love myself"

Chapter 2:
Manifesting Through Love and Gratitude

"I love and accept myself as I am"
"I am grateful for all that is good in my life"

Loving Yourself

The affirmation *"I love and accept myself completely"* will probably either make you smile or cringe, right? Truly loving yourself is not easy and certainly not something you can achieve overnight and it's not easy to "measure". Some of you reading this may not even know if you truly love yourself or not. The best guideline is by looking into a mirror. Can you look straight into your own eyes and say "I love you _____ (your name)"?

Try it and you will probably respond in one of the following ways:

cringing big time

laughing out loud

smiling broadly

wanting to cry

Needless to say, smiling broadly is the one that shows that you *do* love yourself so if you responded this way, well done, congratulations!

The other 3 answers show that you're either not quite there or far from it. Step 1 to solving the issue of not loving yourself, in my opinion, would be to read the afore mentioned book by Louise Hay called *You Can Heal Your Life* (or watch the film of the same name). She encourages what she calls *Mirror Work*.

As you look at yourself straight in the eye and say "I love you" record how you feel. Make a note of the first thoughts that pop into your head. You may well come up with a whole stream of reasons why you shouldn't love yourself. Make a note of these and then find something you *do* love about yourself. If the word "love" is a little intense for you (it was for me in the beginning) then use the word "like". What do you like about yourself? What physical characteristics do you like? What personality traits do you like about yourself? What are the best bits about you?

For example, "I love/like my eyes. I love/like the colour of my eyes and how they shine when I smile"

"I love/like my smile"

"I love/like the way I make my friends laugh"

"I love/like the way I look in my favourite shirt"

"I love/like the way I managed to help my friend _____ the other day"

Find things you do love or like about yourself. Look yourself in the eye and say them to yourself. Make a habit of this. I understand, at first, this may seem a bit weird but it works. Love is contagious. It will spread to other parts of you. You will gradually be able to work in the word *love* instead of *like* and add more things about yourself that you love until you can say *I love you* to your whole self whilst looking straight into your own eyes in the mirror. It is so healing and when you get there you will smile. Broadly. You will feel joy within. Believe me.

The truth is that if you can't truly love yourself, how can you expect anyone else to truly love you?

And if you can't truly love yourself, how can you truly love anyone else? This really is the starting point of healing yourself to happiness.

Giving Gratitude

Giving gratitude is also one of the easiest and simplest ways to manifest the happiness you want in life. I started *counting my blessings* a few years ago by just acknowledging and appreciating my mother, sister and son in my life each day. I used to have a wind chime hanging just outside my front door and as I passed it in the hallway on my way out every morning I used to touch it and say thank you for my closest family members. To be honest I didn't think much about it and I had no idea at the time how powerful this action was going to be.

I got the idea of giving gratitude and counting my blessings during my Reiki class. Finding myself there in that class was a blessing in itself. I had had no intentions of learning Reiki. To be honest I didn't really understand what it was at first. I had wanted to learn reflexology and while checking out courses I saw a course in Holistic Therapies which included reflexology, Swedish massage, aromatherapy and something I'd vaguely heard of called Reiki! I signed up for it.

Looking back I can see clearly how I was led to that Reiki class and my Reiki Master (now a dear friend) as part of my Soul's journey but at the time I was just enjoying a year out from primary teaching thanks to a small but very much appreciated inheritance from my Auntie Joyce. My mother had insisted I save it but I knew my late Auntie Joyce would want me to spend it on following my heart and that's exactly what I did. I followed my heart with a once in a lifetime, dream come true, Safari holiday in Kenya with my son and I was able to take a year out of teaching to study reflexology and other holistic therapies.

So, the Reiki was new to me as were its 5 Principles. The 5 Principles of Reiki have grown to mean so much to me now, or rather I have grown to deeply appreciate them. I wonder how they resonate with you?

Just for today, do not be angry

Just for today, do not worry

Just for today, be grateful

Just for today, work hard

Just for today, be kind to others

Dr Mikao Usui, the founder of Usui Shiki Ryoho Reiki, originally wrote these principles in Japanese. There have been many translations of these principles which, initially seems strange taking into account their brevity. However, the ongoing debates among Reiki practitioners as to the *exact* translation of these 5 simple sentences is testimony to their depth and wisdom and to the diversity of their interpretation. As with many writings, we take from them what we will.

Dr Mikao Usui taught these principles to his students as strategies to apply to life and I want to take this opportunity to raise your awareness to applying these 5 Principles to your life as part of your healing path to happiness. For those of us already aware of these principles, their regular revision is uplifting as they take on greater meaning within us. They make excellent affirmations too, of course!

Just for today, do not be angry

Anger can be and is a very destructive and self-destructive force as it hurts us as well as others. Anger blocks us from love and compassion.

I realise it's easier said than done to just stop being angry and it's best not to suppress the feeling for it to return another time. So finding a way to deal with the feelings of anger when they come is essential. Anger uses a lot of our energy and it is never in alignment with our True path. You need to remind yourself that anger is not your real nature and, as such , it will pass. Try to acknowledge it, witness it and then let it go forever. Welcome calmness. Holding anger in can and will do more harm than good especially to ourselves. Have you never noticed how angry, bitter people tend to look haggard and unhealthy compared to others?

I love this quote from Mark Twain about Anger,

"Anger is an acid that can do more harm to the vessel in which it is stored than to anything on which it is poured."

The second of the 5 Reiki Principles is:

Just for today, do not worry

Worry, like anger will also deplete your vital energy. While anger deals with past and present, worry deals with the perceived future. We usually have no ultimate control over future circumstances anyway so worry is pretty pointless. It's also, like anger, very unhealthy. Some people seem to think worrying about loved ones is a sign of caring but in fact, it projects a negative energy around both the worrier and the person being worried about. If you think about it, worrying doesn't achieve anything positive, only negative. I always tell clients to substitute the word *think* for the word *worry*. You can *think* about a situation, a solution, your friend or family. It's far more positive to *think* about a difficult situation and how you can help solve it. *Thinking* is far more fruitful, productive and positive than *worrying*".

Just for today, be grateful

Here is the third Reiki Principle and the one most relevant to this chapter. If we live in a state of gratitude, appreciating and giving thanks for the many blessings in life that we have, we can help transform negative attitudes and thoughts into positive ones. This, in turn, raises our vibrations and attracts more things for us to be grateful for. This is the seed of abundance!

Just for today, work hard

Of course, these Principles have been translated from their original Japanese and exact meanings can vary. I have come to believe that when you find your Divine Path you actually don't *feel* like you are working hard because you are usually doing something you are passionate and enthusiastic about. I, therefore, think of this Principle more as *Be Active* rather than actually working hard. If the work is in alignment with your True path then it won't feel *hard* to do. Another way to look at this one is basically *Don't be lazy*!

Just for today, be kind to others

The last of the 5 Principles is telling us to show kindness to others. We must honour all living things (including animals and plants) and be tolerant of the way others choose to live their lives.

It is important that we realise and accept that being kind and friendly to everyone must include ourselves of course.

So here concludes the 5 Reiki Principles—simple and to the point. A slight detour maybe but I wanted to share them with you. Back to gratitude. It was at this time I started to appreciate the concept of gratitude and the magnitude of its healing and manifesting abilities.

Slowly, over time, I added more people to my list of blessings to count each morning. Then later, I added things to the list. My good health was one of them, the weather, the birds singing, blue skies, the wonderful girls on my course and the amazing things I was learning. I would look around me as I walked in the street, finding things to be grateful for. It is an excellent practice especially when driving. When you get caught at the lights be grateful for something. Look around you. Find something. It certainly heals road rage. After a while you will find things to be grateful for just flow forth.

Then I started writing them down in a little notebook. The more I did this, the more the Universe gave me to be grateful for. It's all about matching vibrations. If you complain and send out the negative vibrations of complaining, the Universe will match it by giving you more things to complain about. If you send out the positive vibrations of gratitude, Like attracts Like, the Universe has to match it and you will just keep getting more and more things to be grateful for.

One of the main reasons that gratitude is such a simple and easy method of manifesting is because, like affirmations, it can happen in your head, as often as you like. As soon as you wake up, while cleaning your teeth, waiting in a queue, while waiting at the bus stop, while eating etc. Just look around you and find things to be grateful for and just say it, to yourself. Thank you for my morning tea, thank you for the birds singing, thank you for this apple pie, etc.

Some people feel weird because they don't know who they are saying thank you to. Personally I thank the Universe. Some people thank God. You can even thank yourself. If it still feels weird you can change the words to "*I appreciate . . .*" or "*I am grateful for . . .*" then you don't have to think about to whom you are talking but the positive energy of gratitude is still emitting from your energy field. (This is the important thing!)

As I said, for greater impact and effectiveness write your blessings down. I've now got notebooks and journals full of my blessings. I find a quiet spot and a quiet moment. Each page headed with the date and *Today I am Grateful for:*—my lists go on and on. Use your senses. What can you *see* that you're grateful for? What can you *smell*? What can you *hear*? How do you *feel*?

Always include your relationships in your Gratitude Lists, especially those that are troubled. Find something to be grateful for in the people you find difficult. Whatever you focus on is what you will get more of so find something positive to say about those difficult people in your life.

Focus on the good things about the relationship. The bits you want more of. Remember that *energy goes where attention flows.*

And when you make mistakes. Look for the silver lining. You can express gratitude for the lessons you're learning.

If you're poorly or sick be grateful for the bits of you that are healthy. If you're not happy with your body, be grateful for the bits you *are* happy with. This is an amazing tool for learning to love and appreciate your body. It is so easy for us in today's world to dislike our bodies and even actively and verbally (well inside our heads anyway) hate parts of our bodies. Giving gratitude for our bodies and body parts is the easiest way to become more beautiful. Seriously. I'll explain how.

Beautifying Yourself from Within

Masaru Emoto (1943 - 2014) was a Japanese researcher who proved that human consciousness has an effect on the molecular structure of water. Emoto showed that water reacted to positive thoughts and words, and that polluted water could be cleaned through prayer and positive visualization. He found that the purer the water the more beautiful the crystals.

Emoto went on to publish his work entitled Messages from Water, which contains photographs, including the ones below, of ice crystals and their accompanying experiments.

His experiments included exposing water crystals to a selection of photographs, music, words and prayers. Keeping in mind that everything is energy how do you think the water crystals responded?

Love and Gratitude

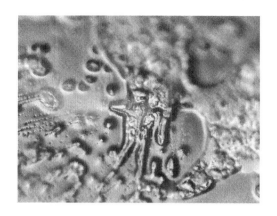

You make me sick
I will kill you

Thank You

You can see that the water crystals responded to love and gratitude by making beautiful formations and to the negative energy of the nasty words by being, well, not so pretty, eh? He did the same with music which also carries energy.

Being exposed to the music of Bach, Beethoven and Mozart made the water crystals really beautiful as did The Beatles song *Yesterday* and John Lennon's *Imagine*. Heavy metal music made the molecules irregular in form and basically ugly.

The prettiest crystal formation, in my opinion, was when exposed to the music of *Edelwise*. My other favourites include the crystals exposed to the word *Truth* and to Martin Luther King's famous *'I have a dream'* speech.

Visit www.masaru-emoto.net/english/water-crystal.html and pick *your* favourites.

Here we have the proof that words, and the thoughts behind them, carry energy. And we can see the profound effects of this energy. Our bodies are made up of 70% water. If we express love, appreciation and gratitude to every part of our body, just imagine how each water molecule within us will turn more beautiful. Don't laugh at this notion. Look at the pictures! It really is true! We can turn every molecule of our bodies beautiful by expressing love and gratitude towards them. And by listening to John Lennon's *Imagine*! How cool is that?

This also explains how *Sound Therapy* works. This is why beauty and massage treatment salons play healing music. The next time you go to a massage salon, listen to the calming music they're playing and imagine all those water molecules within you turning more beautiful and healthier. Healthy is the best form of beauty.

My friend, Sean, told me recently about an experiment he had carried out involving growing rice. The rice was placed in 3 separate containers. The first one was lavished with positive feelings, words and thoughts of love and gratitude. The second one was ignored and neglected completely and the 3rd one was subjected to some nasty energy, words and thoughts.

Over time, and as expected, the first one flourished, the 3rd one didn't and, interestingly, the 2nd one went really bad. This proves that neglect has worse consequences on living organisms than negative attention.

You can see the same effects in plants grown by loving gardeners compared to those tended without such positive emotion or passion. This will also explain why the best gardeners talk to their plants. You can see this same principle in the kitchen too. Have you ever wondered why and how some people can cook so much better than others? Chefs and cooks, who love their work, fill all their ingredients with love and gratitude. They love the process of cooking and fill every dish with the energy of love. This is why their food tastes so good.

I would go as far as to add that my hairdresser does this too. He is passionate about his work and treats me like I am a work of art sitting in that chair. And, more importantly, I leave his salon feeling like a work of art. My husband is a builder who is passionate about construction and design. He built my office with so much love, I feel it, and am grateful for it, every time I walk into it. If you want a job well done, go to someone who is passionate about their work.

I have digressed again. My point is this. We are made up of 50 trillion cells (Bruce Lipton says so and he's a Cellular Biologist!) so it makes sense to me that if we fill each one of those cells (or as many as we can) with *love, gratitude* and *joy* we, too, will be healthier and flourish like the 1st container of rice and we, too, will be healthier and "prettier" like Emoto's water crystals. We, too, can be works of art.

So, as you dry yourself after the shower, as you rub on your moisturiser and as you apply your oils, make up, aftershave etc. tell each part of your body how much you love it. Find a reason why and send love to that part of your body and to the numerous cells of that part of your body. Say *thank you* to them. Don't sit there and laugh. Just do it!

Remember the Law of Attraction means the more *love* and *gratitude* you give to your body the more reasons your body will give you to love it and be grateful for it. It's simple!

With whatever issue you're concerned about find *something* to be grateful for. The Universe will take it from there! So get started with *your* gratitude list. You could treat yourself to a lovely new notebook. Start buying them as presents for your friends and family. I love buying notebooks! Or you could just use loose paper or the back of a receipt. It really doesn't matter where you write your lists. It matters that you write them. Today I am grateful for:—you can start with this book :)

Chapter 3:
Emotional Energy Healing

"I release and forgive the past and I welcome the new into my life"

Releasing Stress

"Unexpressed emotions will never die. They are buried alive and will come forth later in uglier ways."
—Sigmund Freud

It was during my course in Holistic Therapies that I really began to appreciate the importance of releasing stress from our bodies. We had been warned at the start of the course that we would experience laughter and tears in equal measure as we spent day after day giving and receiving the various treatments. It was wonderful to go to college every day and be massaged but as the everyday stresses released from our bodies so did the pent up negative emotions that we had all learned to suppress. As predicted, there was lots of laughter and just as many tears as we all went on this glorious learning journey together. Growing and healing is all about learning and releasing.

For my reflexology qualification I had to have 2 practice clients who were prepared to have a full reflexology session once a week for 10 weeks while I took notes. In that time, amazing changes took place in their lives. We were told to expect the clients to feel rough and want to stop after about 4 or 5 sessions and sure enough, this was the case. It was referred to as a *healing crisis*. In other modalities we call it *processing* but, either way, it happens when suppressed and trapped emotions are releasing from the body. If you think about how much stress the body actually went through when it originally felt these emotions, and often for long periods at a time, it is no wonder that the body should feel *emotionally wobbly,* as I like to phrase it, as these emotions release.

I try and explain it by comparing our bodies to a metal spoon. Imagine the spoon handle has been bent over itself. The point where the metal bends will be weak. If you want to straighten the spoon handle again ie: put it back into equilibrium, you will need to put further pressure on that same point where the spoon bent the first time. You would assert this further pressure slowly and carefully until the spoon is back in alignment. Well, we are the same. Sometimes, healing can be challenging and we can feel weak and vulnerable. We cannot release *emotions* without feeling *emotional*.

Emotional healing affects people differently and some people embrace it more than others. One of my reflexology practice clients started to completely turn her life around during that 10 weeks and afterwards. Her confidence grew, she stood taller with improved posture and she got herself the job which she had only dreamed about before. You could say this was all coincidence and that she was going to change in this way anyway. Maybe she was. But I later saw similar changes in another client after a course of holistic treatments. She gained in confidence and turned her life around. Maybe people seek holistic therapies and treatments when they are at a certain point in their lives. After all, we are already breaking away from the victim role by allowing ourselves the opportunity to benefit from such therapies.

I believe that making the time and money to spend on ourselves in the first place, in itself, plays an important role in our healing. It says "*I am worth it*" and "*I deserve to take care of myself*". This is all part of the *whole* when it comes to holistic and emotional healing.

Of course, the good old fashioned method of emotional healing is Counselling and I have always valued its importance. Even though counselling can be a little hit and miss at times, definitely long winded and usually calls for a whole box of tissues, it *does* work. Talking through our feelings helps us put them into perspective. Especially with a qualified counsellor who can ask the right questions and hold a secure, safe and nurturing environment for us to "*let it all out*". A good counsellor will be able to pick up on our choice of wording and help identify the limiting subconscious beliefs behind these words. This is where Neuro-Linguistic Programming comes in. I first came across NLP when training in management. It is used widely in the Business world to help achieve success.

According to Wikipedia Neuro-linguistic programming (NLP) is

"*an approach to communication, personal development, and psychotherapy created by Richard Bandler and John Grinder in California, United States in the 1970s ... a model for gathering information and challenging a client's language and underlying thinking."*

In my opinion, NLP is a very interesting subject and one that is relevant to all aspects of life. We can learn a lot about people from their choice of words, we can influence and motivate others with our choice of words and above all, as we have already seen with affirmations, we can change and heal a lot about ourselves with our choice of words.

However, when it comes to releasing stress and trapped emotions I have found some amazing modalities which, not only have changed my life and the lives of my clients, but that you can learn to do yourself. I believe that our greatest power is within us and real self healing comes from understanding, appreciating and tapping into this power. But before I tell you about these amazing energy healing methods, I want to first clarify exactly what I mean by the term *"trapped emotion"*.

What is a Trapped Emotion?

To understand what a trapped emotion is, we must first understand that *everything* is energy. Well, we don't need to understand it exactly but to recognise it as the scientific fact that it is. We need to accept that everything is energy. Moving, vibrating energy. In addition to everything being vibrating energy, it all vibrates at different frequencies. When it comes to these frequencies, it's a case of, the higher the better. So there is truth in the popular phrases *"good vibes"* and *"bad vibes"*. Good vibes being things that make us feel better and raise our vibrations and bad vibes being the ones that lower our vibrations and leave us feeling worse. Positive feelings give us *good vibes* and we need them if we are to heal ourselves.

Even abstract things, are made of energy and have vibrations. Namely our *thoughts* and *emotions*. When we think a thought we are actually letting the energy of that thought pass through our bodies. Good thoughts are higher in vibrations and therefore healthier for us which is why *positive thinking* is such a big deal. Likewise, when we feel an emotion, the energy of that emotion is passing through our body. Good emotions are vibrating at higher frequencies and therefore raise our vibrations and negative emotions vibrating at lower frequencies, therefore, lower our vibrations.

The point is that when we feel something ie. an emotion, it is in the form of energy passing through our bodies. Sometimes, in the case of severe trauma, heartbreak or bereavement, for example, we do not or cannot fully process the emotion and our bodies shut down. Perhaps we just go numb or we deny ourselves the right to feel that way and we bury the feeling deep inside. You hear about people struck with grief who go on *auto pilot*. Well, it may help them to function better at the time but that's a big ball of negative energy to be buried in the body. We need to process the emotion and get it out. If left unprocessed it will stay in the body. It will lodge somewhere in the body and block the natural healing flow of energy. This negative emotion, in turn, will attract, by its frequency, more negative emotional energy of that same frequency. This ball of emotional energy has to go somewhere and this, in itself, is an interesting point which I will come on to in just a moment. But first I want to make it clear that we *all* have trapped emotions. Some people can get quite defensive about the concept of them having trapped emotions. Almost as if it is some kind of inadequacy. As if it displays some kind of weakness within them. After all, it would be impossible to go through life without feeling emotions, wouldn't it?

When we think about our most traumatic times it is easy to understand that we may have trapped negative emotions. For example, the feeling of rejection or betrayal after a relationship break up or the emotion of abandonment when our mother doesn't defend us as a child against a violent step father. But trapped emotions can also be from far less significant events. A 3 year old who has lost his favourite toy could trap emotions of loss, anxiety or despair. Or a small child getting lost in a shop could trap emotions of panic and we have all experienced these things.

We can also have compounded trapped emotions. Once we have trapped an emotion, the next time we feel that same emotion it compounds with the existing trapped emotion that wasn't processed and makes the feeling of the emotion more intense. This can cause us to overreact in certain situations as we are responding to the pain and effects of the original emotion as well as the one experienced in the present moment. Counsellors commonly call this concept "Big Bells Little Bells" when a small emotion in the present triggers a larger trapped emotion from within. These compound trapped emotions can also make us even more vulnerable to trapping that emotion again in the future. Being able to release such compound trapped emotions is therefore such a necessity and a blessing.

Where, in the body, does the negative energy go?

If the body already has a weak area then the new negative energy will most commonly find its way there, creating a nest of emotions. Over time it creates a bigger and bigger blockage to the naturally flowing positive energy that is trying to pass around the body. This blockage then creates an imbalance where pain, mal-function and disease can occur. If there is no apparent weak area then it becomes quite interesting where the negative emotion chooses to reside. The actual location within the body is usually relevant to the emotions being trapped.

Traditional Chinese medicine, which has been practiced for more than five thousand years, classifies five major organ systems that are each associated with particular emotions. The five major organ systems involve pairs of organs and an associated emotion. The liver and gallbladder are associated with anger. The heart and small intestine are associated with joy. The spleen and stomach are associated with over-thinking, worry and nervousness. The lungs and large intestine are associated with grief and the kidney and bladder are associated with fear.

So if you trap emotions of grief, for example, the mal function and disease could manifest in your lungs. Pent up, unexpressed emotions of anger could cause problems in your liver. Fear can often make people need the toilet and excessive worriers often end up with stomach ulcers. It really does make sense when you think about it.

Louise Hay took this a step further and her very first book, in the 1970's, was, in fact, a list of symptoms and their associated emotional cause. This list can be found at the back of her afore mentioned book, *You Can Heal Your Life*. Next to each symptom and the emotional cause of that symptom Louise offers an affirmation to counteract the underlying cause. It's very interesting to see the relationship between our symptoms and our emotional state. Some of them can be very logical. For example shoulder problems reflect the perception of carrying a burden. Sore throats relate to problems with communicating and expressing ourselves especially with holding in anger. Bedwetting relates to fear. Usually of a parent especially the father. Breast issues relate to nurturing others before ourselves. Not wanting to hear something in your life can cause ear problems and not wanting to see something in your life can cause eye problems. Where we carry weight is also relevant to our trapped emotions. Belly fat can relate to a lack of emotional self-nourishment. Thighs relate to hidden hurt and anger at the father. Warts are small eruptions of emotional anger or irritation. I could go on but you get the gist. I wonder how many of these resonate with you and those around you. It can be a real A-ha moment when you first realise this connection. Louise Hay, along with others in her field, has made a link between cancer and unresolved trapped emotions of resentment. I started looking at cases I knew about and it makes sense to me.

Of course, holding onto such emotions and/or ways of thinking is something we are not aware we are doing at first. You have to remember these emotions are buried deep and our subconscious beliefs are, just that, subconscious. Many people can get quite indignant when they are told, in effect, that they are responsible, whether directly or indirectly, wittingly or unwittingly, for their own illnesses. But I'm afraid it's true. Very true. And the sooner we can take responsibility for our illnesses and problems, the sooner we can do something about them. The sooner we can work on releasing the harmful blockages, the sooner we can heal ourselves to health and happiness.

Emotional Freedom Technique (EFT)

I don't recall exactly when or how I first came across EFT. It was probably via the internet. But I do remember being excited and motivated to learn more about it.

EFT was created by Gary Craig, in the early 1990's and he is still active in sharing his love of EFT with the world and has made learning about EFT free and easily available via his website at www.emofree.com.

There have been a number of people since then who have written books on the subject of EFT and who have contributed to spreading its popularity. More recently and very successfully has been Nick Ortner with his book called The Tapping Solution published by Hay House.

Emotional Freedom Technique, EFT for short, works on similar principles to other energy healing modalities in as far as it uses pressure points, as in acupuncture, and the body's meridian lines as in Reiki and reflexology. It involves gentle tapping with your fingertips to stimulate certain pressure points on the face and chest and releases the trapped energy along the meridian lines. It can be used to release and heal physical and emotional symptoms, whether the result of a traumatic event, an addiction, pain, illness, anxiety, etc.

Our bodies are naturally designed to self heal. It is only when we experience blocks to this natural healing that distress and disease occurs. It's not a case of adding the healing. It's a case of removing the blocks and that's exactly what EFT does.

Even though there are numerous books and videos available demonstrating this amazing technique, I wanted to learn from a professional in person so I could ask questions and gain confidence. I checked out training courses in becoming an EFT Practitioner and found Don Ely in East Grinstead, Sussex. The dates of his courses weren't convenient for me but, sensing my enthusiasm and motivation, he offered to teach me on a one to one. I had recently finished my Reiki course so I was very open to the theories and ideas behind the field of Energy Psychology.

In order to explain the technique Don asked me to think of a personal issue I could work on. I immediately chose *"weight"* as an issue mainly because it was one that he could *see* and, at about 90 kilos at the time, it was an issue I couldn't deny.

Well, I really wasn't prepared for what happened next. Within a few rounds of the tapping I felt overwhelming feelings of guilt come up. Guilt at not having been a better Mum to my son in his early years. The feeling seemed to come from absolutely nowhere. It was really weird because my conscious mind wasn't aware at all that I felt like that. In fact, although things had been tough in the beginning, my conscious mind thought I had done well as a Mum. But here I was, in Don's office crying like a baby about my son not deserving to have such a terrible mother. I was quite inconsolable and quite in shock at the power of this emotion. Well that trapped emotion certainly came out. Don professionally counselled me back to coherence and we discussed the ins and outs of this amazing technique. I learned so much that day. My interest in energy psychology just got greater.

I didn't notice the weight loss at first. It was gradual yet consistent. I didn't consciously change my diet or exercise routine. I just simply lost weight. Around a kilo a week from that day on until I'd lost over 20 kilos. It felt and still feels glorious to be at such a healthy weight. I am convinced that weight is an emotional issue.

One of the reasons that I am such a big fan of EFT is that it can be learned and used by ourselves. It empowers us with our own healing and that is what this book is all about. Healing *Yourself* to Happiness. Here's how.

EFT is one of the only modalities where we actually focus on the problem rather than the result. But only to start with.

Firstly, I advise you to sit somewhere quiet and comfortable where you won't be disturbed, either on your own or with someone you feel comfortable working with. You could play some calming music, light a candle, burn some oils, whatever helps you relax and focus. Take a few deep, full breaths and set your intention to heal.

We start with setting the scene so to speak by using the *karate chop* tap first. While tapping the outer edge of one hand with the finger tips of the other hand say

" Even though I'm overweight, I love and accept myself completely"

I am using the example I gave during my first session here but obviously you're going to use your own.

eg "Even though I feel scared (of dogs), I love and accept myself completely"

"Even though I feel anxious, worried, pain (where), resentment, grief, unable to sleep, etc I love and accept myself completely". Say this a few times (at least x 3)

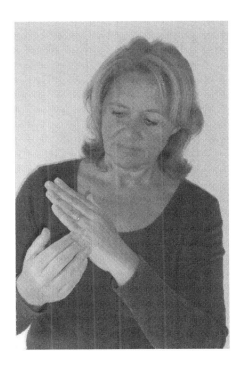

Then moving to the inner end of an eyebrow, still with the finger tips (you can use 2, 3 or all 4 finger tips, whichever is most comfortable for you) tap whilst repeating the set up phrase,

"Even though I'm overweight, I love and accept myself completely"

Speak slowly and with intention. You only need to say the phrase once at each tapping point but you will be tapping a few times.

Then move to the outer edge of the eye. Repeat the phrase.

Then move to the cheek bone under the eye. Repeat the phrase again. You can miss out the "overweight" part, or whatever issue you're focussing on, when it feels right to do so.

The next point is under the nose just above the top lip. Repeat, *"I love and accept myself completely"*

Then under the bottom lip on the fold of the chin. Repeat.

Then just under the clavicle, either side, it doesn't matter. Whichever is more comfortable.

On the fleshy bit. The clavicle is the bone going from your neck to your shoulder.

After this, a bit like a monkey, tap under your arm on the bra line (whether you wear one or not!)

Finally, up to the top of your head and tap on the crown of your head.

"I love and accept myself completely"

Some people start with the point at the top of the head. Either way it works.

Now you can go straight into a second and third round of tapping or you can stop after each round and refocus. I always suggest placing your hands on your chest and breathe deeply. What is the very first thought or feeling that comes to mind?

If it's a feeling then add it to your next phrase, *"Even though I feel_____, I love and accept myself completely"* Complete another round (or 2 or 3) of tapping using the new found feeling. When you get to the top of the head again, place your hands on your chest and breathe deeply again. What's your first thought again? Don't dismiss this first thought or feeling. This is where the healing lies. Keep going paying attention to each change in feeling and each thought that comes up.

It may well seem completely irrelevant and unrelated but it won't be. It will be the underlying cause of your problem coming up. If you feel like crying please do. That is the release and the healing that your body is looking for. Let it all out.

Keep going with more rounds of tapping until you feel positive feelings come up and until you feel calm and relaxed again. All is well.

Here are the tapping points again to help you.

Inside End of An Eyebrow

Outside Edge of the Eye

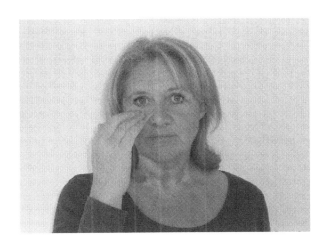

Under the Eye on the Cheek Bone

Under the Nose, Above the Top Lip

Under the Bottom Lip on the Fold of the Chin

On the Fleshy Part, Just Under the Clavicle

Under the Arm on the Bra Line

On the Top of the Head

Releasing emotions, however we choose to do it, can leave us feeling tired and drained. Be kind to yourself during this time. You will probably sleep like a log and the next day you'll wake up feeling lighter, brighter and healthier. You'll soon think of other issues and situations you want to heal. Try it with whatever issues you come up with. You'll be surprised where it will lead you. And you will be relieved of the emotional healing it brings. Good Luck!

The Emotion Code and The Body Code

The Emotion Code and The Body Code are, for me, *The Big Ones*. They are the easiest and quickest methods I have found that, not only I have benefitted from the most, but also the methods I use most with my clients.

The Emotion Code is an amazing new energy healing system and book devised and written by Dr Bradley Nelson. A holistic chiropractic physician and medical intuitive, "Dr. Brad" is one of the world's foremost experts in the emerging fields of bio-energetic medicine and energy psychology. The Emotion Code works on the same principles as other holistic energy work in as far as it's based on the fact that everything is energy and its aim is to release trapped emotions (energy) from within the body which cause energy blockages which in turn cause physical and emotional issues.

Furthermore, to complicate matters we also have "inherited trapped emotions" which are basically passed onto us at the time of conception from either biological parent. Our parents too, could have inherited the trapped emotion from *their* parents and it is common to find these inherited trapped emotions spanning back through the generations. Releasing these inherited emotions can often bring powerful healing and relief to ailments. It's almost as if they have built up strength and impact as they have passed down the gene line and it is important to note that once released they have been released from the *whole* gene line forwards as well as backwards. The thought of inheriting negative energy from our parents is always easier to handle than the thought of passing it onto our children so it is comforting to understand that once released it is released from the whole biological family.

The ability to heal ourselves from inherited issues is mind blowing and an area that, thanks to the work of Dr Bruce Lipton, is now referred to as Epigenetics. Allow me to digress to expand on this a moment.

Epigenetics is defined by Google as,

"the study of changes in organisms caused by modification of gene expression rather than alteration of the genetic code itself."

Dr Bruce Lipton explained how his research revealed the science of epigenetics.

Quoting from his website,

"I placed one stem cell into a culture dish, and it divided every ten hours. After two weeks, there were thousands of cells in the dish, and they were all genetically identical, having been derived from the same parent cell. I divided the cell population and inoculated them in three different culture dishes.

"Next, I manipulated the culture medium—the cell's equivalent of the environment—in each dish. In one dish, the cells became bone, in another, muscle, and in the last dish, fat. This demonstrated that the genes didn't determine the fate of the cells because they all had the exact same genes. The environment determined the fate of the cells, not the genetic pattern. So if cells are in a healthy environment, they are healthy. If they're in an unhealthy environment, they get sick."

Clearly this shows that our environments and how we respond to them is the key to our health. In Chapter 5 we will look further at how our beliefs in inheriting ill-health is what causes the ill-health and not the actual genes but for now, back to the Emotion Code.

With the Emotion Code the negative trapped emotions are quickly identified using kinesiology (muscle testing) and a chart of emotions created by Dr Nelson. Kinesiology is a recognised method for determining positive and negative responses from the body and is commonly used by therapists to identify food allergies and intolerances as well as ascertaining suitable oils and applications for treatment purposes. Because muscle testing is such an important part of Self Healing, I have dedicated the next chapter to showing you how to do it.

Once the trapped emotion has been identified it can be released by running a magnet along the governing meridian line of the body. The governing meridian line runs from the centre of our top lip up, over the nose, and up over the forehead and crown of the head and all the way down the back and spine. When doing it to yourself, you will soon find out you have to stop half way. No worries. This is fine. It's enough.

Personally, I use a Nikken MagDuo magnet (see Reference list) but any magnet will do. You can even use a fridge magnet. In fact, we are magnetic, so you can just use your fingertips. In fact, the more you do this kind of work, the more you can just use the power of intention but to begin with a magnet is good.

For me, The Emotion Code was a logical and practical progression from EFT and, unlike conventional counselling and EFT, there is no need for the box of tissues! We don't need to dwell on the emotional events that caused the trapped emotions. We just identify them and release them. There is sometimes, however, a period of processing (usually a day or two) where the individual can feel "emotionally wobbly" as the emotions fully release from the body. The healing achieved with this method is amazing. It's quick, effective and thorough and it is something you can easily learn to do yourself by reading the book.

The Body Code is an extension of The Emotion Code where Dr Bradley Nelson has compiled a whole series of mind maps covering our entire body's systems. You can buy the program from the Healers Library website. Again, using kinesiology (muscle testing) you can navigate your way to finding the underlying causes of any symptom. It really is a fully comprehensive system. With this system I found that my mercury fillings were causing toxicity within my body. I have since had them safely changed to non-toxic ones. I was also able to balance my underactive thyroid gland allowing me to become drug free for the first time in years. I have used this method to heal panic attacks, nightmares, anxiety and food intolerances and much more and that's just in myself. The list is really extensive with what I've seen healed in my friends, family and clients.

"After twenty-some years and thousands of patients, I'm convinced that trapped emotions are at the basis of almost everything from phobias and anxiety attacks to cancers and fibromyalgia. The good news is that by clearing these trapped emotions, the symptoms of the disease or condition become noticeably better and often the disease or condition itself completely disappears."
—Dr Bradley Nelson

I totally agree with the above quote by Dr Brad but we must be very careful when answering the question of what exactly can be healed with The Emotion Code and The Body Code so as not to be misleading. It is important to understand that every body is very different both physically and emotionally. We are the physical and emotional result of our own experiences, events, trapped emotions, inherited trapped emotions, beliefs, and thoughts. No two people have all of these factors the same so therefore no two people can be healed in the same way. The main cause of disease is from trapped emotions and other negative energy within the body and we all have different trapped emotions and negative energy from our different experiences so our healing will follow a path unique to us.

I have seen, for example, the underlying cause of migraine headaches being 2 or 3 single trapped emotions in one person yet in another it has taken us more sessions, and a windy road, to get the same relief. With this form of energy healing we never know where we are going to be led as everyone's subconscious is unique and sometimes the underlying cause of an issue is something we could never have imagined.

In addition to this, it is common for symptoms we are not focusing on to be relieved whilst working on something completely different. In other words, the underlying causes of one symptom can often be the underlying cause of another, seemingly unrelated, symptom. So it can be seen that no two people will follow the same healing path for the same problem and it is because of this that we cannot say how many sessions will be needed to relieve a certain issue.

The Emotion Code and The Body Code work with energy imbalances and not with the names of diseases that have been given by the medical profession so it can be misleading to connect our healing work with specifically named diseases.

We prefer to work with symptoms rather than medically named diseases.

The Heart Wall

The Heart Wall is an energetic wall we subconsciously place around our hearts to protect us from negative feelings. We can all relate to the phrase Once Bitten Twice Shy. And when we get hurt again and again we reinforce this wall around our hearts and start not caring. We become desensitised to pain and heartache. This can be seen in victims of bullying, domestic violence and those falling for the wrong partner again and again. The Heart Wall helps us not to feel pain, heartache, humiliation and other negative emotions which is great but they work both ways and prevent us from feeling true love, joy and happiness too! Releasing the Heart Wall allows positive feelings to enter, and exit, the heart. This gives such a sense of peace and joy and can really change a person's life. By the Law of Attraction if you present to the world a closed and protected heart you will attract others to you who have closed, protected hearts. In contrast, present to the world a heart radiating love, peace and joy and you will attract others who radiate these emotions.

Clients usually report feeling lighter and freer and that they can see things more clearly once their Heart Wall has been removed. They often have difficulty in describing how they feel but they report that they smile more, notice the nature around them more and are open to receiving. This is why, in my opinion, releasing the Heart Wall is the first and most important step in Energy Healing. It opens up the heart to allow more healing to occur.

In his book, The Emotion Code, Dr Brad explains how anyone can use this method. It is a Self Healing technique. All you need is a regular fridge magnet and to be able to muscle test. However, you may want to invest in a session with a professional just to see what it's all about first. I did just that. It's the best way to learn more about each modality. With The Emotion Code you will find that it can be done over distance, by proxy as they call it. I understand that this seems a bit weird at first but it is no less effective and very much more practical. It means you can find a practitioner that suits you from anywhere in the world and you can have your healing session done over the internet. In fact, with remote sessions, you don't even need to be online with the practitioner while they do the session. This usually poses the following

Frequently Asked Question of how does Energy Healing work over distance.

How does Energy Healing work over distance?

The easy answer to this frequently asked question is that *"We are all connected"*. However, this reply often produces the other frequently asked question of *"How are we all connected?"*

Firstly, to understand how we are all connected, we need to understand, again, that everything is energy. This concept is, I realise, a difficult one to get our heads round, especially as most of us will be sitting on what seems like a solid chair at the moment but, nonetheless, it remains a well documented scientific fact. *Everything* is energy. Not only is everything energy but that energy is, as I have said before, vibrating at various different frequencies. I hope not to sound too repetitive here but this is such an important part of Self Healing, it needs to be taken on board. The Law of Attraction (*Plato—"likes tend toward likes"* circa 391 BC) explains that whatever frequency we give out, we will receive, which is why positive things gravitate towards positive people and vice versa. Whatever we focus our minds on (in other words our thoughts) we will receive and/or become. That is because what we are receiving matches the frequency of our thoughts. If you have 2 people, one full of positivity and the other down in the dumps, after a while they will find a common frequency. Either the positive one will feel worse (in effect they have been drained of their positive energy) or the miserable one will feel better. We all have people, places and things that make us feel better, that raise our vibrations, such as good friends, the beach, sunrises, pets, our favourite armchair, etc So this shows we can actually see and feel the energy around us on an everyday level.

So, how does this apply over distance? Well the roots to this answer lie in Quantum Physics and with 2 main Quantum theories in particular. The first one being that of *Non-locality* (which Einstein referred to as "*spooky action at a distance*") and the second being that of *Entanglement*. Now, I for one, am no Quantum Physicist and I'm guessing not many people reading this are either so I'm not going to even attempt to get into the nitty gritty of these Scientific concepts and the evidence they provide but, please feel free to research them should you be interested to learn more. In short, it has been seen that what affects one particle in one locality also affects another, seemingly separate particle (atom, photon, molecule … energy) in another locality. The Entanglement concept is seen more commonly in new mums who can *sense* when their babies need them or with twins who can *sense* the feelings of each other.

I will, however, again quote the internationally recognised cell biologist and leader in bridging science and spirit, Dr Bruce Lipton PhD, who has, in my opinion, summed it all up beautifully in the 2nd chapter of his book "*The Honeymoon Effect*" (2013) titled appropriately Good Vibrations,

"… once a quantum particle interacts (or in quantum language, "entangles") with another particle, no matter how many miles apart they are, (that is nonlocal), their mechanical states remain coupled. If, for example, one particle's rotational spin is clockwise, its entangled twin's rotational spin is the opposite, counter-clockwise…. No matter how much distance separates them, when the polarity or the rotation of one particle's spin changes, the polarity or rotation of its twin changes simultaneously as well, even if one is in Paris and the other is in Beijing."

I cannot feasibly or legally quote the whole chapter here but it is, in my opinion after considerable research into this phenomenon, the best explanation to us lay people that I have found to date. This book is available to buy online so I urge anyone still struggling with this question to invest in it. (The book also continues to explain how to keep the romance alive in your relationships—hence the title)

When healing over distance (or indeed carrying out a scientific experiment to prove the above theories) one needs to hold focused thought about what they are doing. Energy healers call it *Intention* but its purpose goes back to the fact that thoughts are energy and positive thoughts attract like and, then, that inter connectedness that we all have becomes stronger.

I'm not sure how well this has answered the question for you. I can only explain it as I see it and as I have stated earlier, I am no scientist but for those of you still not sure, I have to ask the question, "Why not just believe?" After all, I do not really understand electricity but I know, believe and expect the light to come on when I flick the switch. I do not really understand how the internet works but I know, believe and expect some answers when I search stuff. And there are millions of people, maybe you're one of them (?) who don't really understand the chemistry behind their prescription drugs yet still *believe* and *expect* them to work.

To quote Bruce Lipton again,

"Once we accept the fact that we are fundamentally energetic beings inextricably connected to the vast, dynamic energetic field we are part of, we can no longer view ourselves as powerless, isolated individuals."

In other words, we are all connected and we have power within this energy connection of ours. There are many ways in which we can use this energy connection to help ourselves and others. There are many Energy Healing modalities out there. I have loved and benefitted from researching a number of them. Reiki, Quantum Touch, Theta healing, Hypnotherapy and many more. You have to find which ones you are drawn to and which ones resonate with you. In this chapter I have covered the ones that strike a chord with me most. The ones that you can do for yourself. But if it's healing you want then you have nothing to lose by trying out these different energy methods. Try with a professional first. Especially if you are feeling sceptical. If I can't persuade you to believe first in order to see, you can try these methods out, see the results and then believe. Either way, it's all about the emotional healing. Once you have established that you can use these methods to heal yourself financially too! And your love life! That will raise your Happiness even more!

Now onto the muscle testing which will help you with this.

Chapter 4:
Muscle Testing

"I lovingly listen to my body's messages"

Sway Test

We now understand that everything is energy. Our bodies, our thoughts, our emotions, our food and all substances are in fact energy. Energies (thoughts, substances etc.) that are good and positive for our body make our muscles strengthen and those which are bad or negative for our body weaken our muscles.

Here is a little test you can do yourself to prove this point. It's called The Sway Test.

Stand comfortably with your feet shoulder width apart, drop your shoulders and relax. They call this position Mountain Pose in Yoga. Breathe deeply and focus. Close your eyes and think of something or someone you love, a happy experience for you, the word love and notice how your body moves. Does is lean forwards?

This is because these thoughts are good for your body.

Now try the same with a negative thought or word. Stand in Mountain pose. Relax, focus, close your eyes and think of a violent experience, a nasty person and scene and the word hate. How does your body react? Does it start to fall backwards?

This is because these thoughts are negative for your body and not congruent with your body.

Now try holding a piece of fresh fruit to your chest. Stand up straight. Relax. Focus. Breathe in and ask yourself , "is this fruit good for my body?"

Which way do you sway?

Do the same with a packet of cigarettes, for example, and feel the difference. Ask yourself, "Are these cigarettes good for my body?" What happens? Which way do you sway?

Try with other foods you have around you. Bread is a good one to test. So many people are sensitive to gluten these days. You'll be surprised how many foods you considered healthy are in fact not good for your body. It's all very well to follow supposed healthy diets but only you have access to what *your* body really needs. Just because a food item is healthy for others, doesn't mean your body wants or needs it. Especially in today's world where we have no idea how a lot of our food is treated. Broccoli is supposedly healthy for us, for example, but not when it's covered in insecticide. Only by muscle testing the food on your plate can you be sure you're eating what your body really needs.

Self Muscle Testing

There are a number of ways we can test this change in our muscle strength. Here are some of my favourites. See which one you prefer.

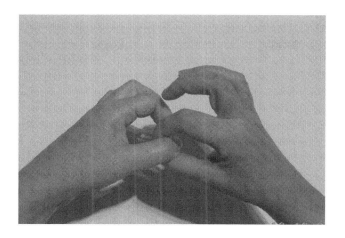

This *"Ring in Ring"* method is an easy and practical way to feel the strength of your muscles. Place your fingers in interlocking rings as shown. Using both hands gently try and pull your fingers apart. You are not necessarily trying to break the ring or force your fingers free from the other hand. You are merely sensing whether your muscles have responded positively by strengthening or negatively by weakening. Ask yourself some questions you already know the answer to. Start with your name for example. State clearly, *My name is* _____. Then pull gently on your fingers and make a mental note of the strength of your muscles holding the interlocking rings together. Now say a false name that means nothing to you, for example *My name*

is Jo Bloggs. Gently pull on the fingers. What happens? Are they the same strength? Are they weaker?

Try with some other factual questions. Use your age. *I am _____ years old.* Now try with a false age. What happens?

It is important to practice with factual questions. You can't ask questions that are debatable or a matter of opinion. And always use a false name that means nothing to you when practicing. If you use a loved one's name then your feelings of love for that person will flood around your body and make your muscles stronger. It is also interesting to note what happens when we change our names. When I married my Mr Right my body immediately resonated with my new name although it did still test strong for my maiden name too. It still tests strong for both but is noticeably stronger for my married name which I take as yet another sign that I married the right person!

Here are some other methods of self muscle testing. With a little practice you can begin to sense your muscles strengthening and weakening in a number of ways.

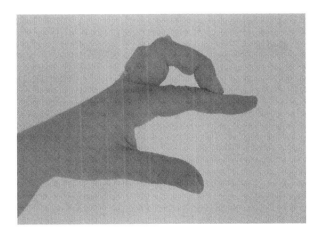

The first one here is nicknamed *Hans Solo* because you can do it with one hand which can be very practical for many reasons including when holding food items in the other hand. With your fingers straight, place your middle finger on top of your index finger like shown. Gently push down with the middle finger on top and test the strength of the muscles in the index finger as it either resists the push (positive response) or bends down under the strength of it (negative response).

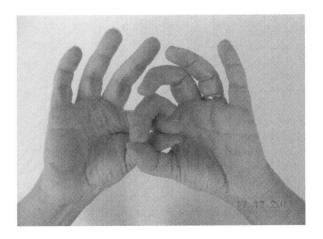

The second picture here shows the *Pinch method*. First make a ring with the fingers of one hand and then place the index finger and thumb of the other hand into the ring of the first hand. Ask your question and gently prise your index finger and thumb apart. Does the ring of the first hand come apart? It is the muscle strength in the ring that you are testing here. If the ring easily breaks as you pull your index finger and thumb apart then that's a negative answer. If the ring stays firmly closed then that's a positive answer.

Every *body* is different and stress can cause us to develop food intolerances so what is healthy for one person may not be healthy for another.

Food intolerances are often a sign that our body just wants a break from a certain food's energy. If your body has indicated that a particular food isn't good for you, you can then ask how long you should avoid it for? More than a week? Does your body say yes or no? More than 2 weeks? What do your muscles say? Remember, if they are strong that's a yes. If they are weaker, then that's a no answer. More than a month? No? Then ask three weeks? You can use this questioning technique to calculate exactly what length of time you should avoid the food. After this time, it should be ok to gradually introduce the food item into your diet again. The body often just wants to cleanse itself of the energy of that food or rebalance it. If you only eat foods that test positive to your muscle testing your body will very soon feel so much better and more energised. It will really thank you. This, in itself, is often the best cure for IBS and other digestive problems.

An interesting point to note here is that we often develop addictions to the food items we are most intolerant to. Sugar is the best example of this as are alcohol and chocolate. People that love bread are often gluten intolerant. In these cases it may be comforting to learn that maybe you don't have to give these favourite substances up forever. You can avoid them for a period of time (muscle test how long) and enjoy them, in moderation, again afterwards. Try it and see.

Muscle Testing Others

To muscle test someone else you need to position yourself as in the picture here. Put one hand on the shoulder for support and using 2 fingers just up the arm a fraction from the wrist joint, gently press downwards. The person being tested needs to resist but not as if in an arm wrestle! Just enough to establish a *normal* level of strength.

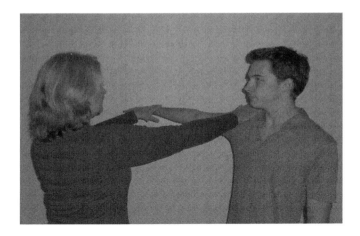

As with self muscle testing, the aim is to simply measure muscle strength so ask an obvious question first as a base test. Get the person being tested to say their name *My name is* _____ as you did for yourself before, and push down on the arm just enough to feel the strength of the muscles. Get the person being tested to say a false name now and push with the *same* force and get the person being tested to use the *same* level of resistance and see what happens. Done correctly you should be able to detect that the muscles have weakened and the arm should move downwards more easily under the pressure of your 2 fingers. You can now get the person being tested to hold items of food and other substances in their other hand or close to their chest and get them to ask themselves "*Is this food/substance good for my body*". Gently push the arm downwards and see if their muscles have strengthened or weakened. Again, this may take some practice so don't give up.

Communicating with your Subconscious Mind and Higher Self

Muscle testing is not only the best way to check the foods you eat, but it is also an amazing way to actually communicate with your subconscious mind and Higher Self. We can get so many answers this way. For example, in Chapter 1 when we were looking at affirmations, I said you can muscle test to see which ones you need most. When you read or recite an affirmation your body can *feel* the energy of the words and the thoughts behind them. If your body instinctively agrees with the words and thoughts being expressed it will respond positively and your muscles will be strong. If the words, and thoughts associated with those words, are not congruent with your subconscious mind, then your body will react by weakening and your muscle testing will prove negative. Did you make a list of affirmations to work on from Chapter 1? Try muscle testing them to see whether your subconscious mind believes them or not. Maybe there were others that you weren't sure about. You can go back and check them now by saying the affirmation clearly and muscle testing yourself while you think about the meaning of the words you are saying. See how you get on. Maybe you need to add some more affirmations to your list. Over time, as you repeat your affirmations, you can muscle test them to see if your subconscious mind has accepted them. Check whether they have become part of your subconscious belief system. If they have, make sure you celebrate and give gratitude!

Chapter 5: Belief Healing

"I am ready and willing to release negative belief and behavioural patterns"

What is a limiting subconscious belief?

We program our minds from a very young age usually from our parents, teachers and other significant adults in our lives at the time. We are totally unaware that we do it and for this reason we are often unaware that we are limiting ourselves with such beliefs. Thought and therefore belief, is energy and, as always, the Universe will match it. If you were told as a small child, for example, that you didn't deserve something, that you weren't good enough or if you felt unloved and unlovable, by continuing to believe this, your beliefs will make it true and the Universe will bring you more situations where you don't feel deserving, good enough or loved. By installing statements (affirmations) of *"I deserve ..."* and *"I am worthy ..." "I am loved ..."*

etc the Universe will match this and give you situations whereby you feel deserving, good enough and loved. This can, and does, change people's lives around as we build so much of our lives on our beliefs especially the beliefs we have about ourselves.

Our beliefs are the foundation of who we are. These beliefs are the result of this lifelong programming, and represent a powerful influence on human behaviour. It is from our beliefs that we form attitudes about the world and ourselves, and from these attitudes we develop behaviours and habits. Beliefs have far-reaching consequences, both positive and negative, in every area of our life. They affect our mood, relationships, job, self-esteem and even physical health. It is so important that we learn how to identify the beliefs that are limiting us by not serving us and how to change them into beliefs that support us.

The ability to perform effectively, both personally and professionally is profoundly affected by such beliefs as *"I am good enough"*, *"I am safe"*, *"I am worthy and deserving"*, *"I am prosperous"* or *"I am lovable"*. Beliefs establish the limits of what we can achieve.

As Henry Ford famously once said,

"If you believe you can or if you believe you can't ... you're right!"

The Law of Attraction is always working whether we like it or not. If our beliefs about ourselves are negative, they will be attracting more negative circumstances into our lives. It's like a vicious cycle that needs to be broken. Fortunately, once we know this, we can break it. By choosing to believe positive beliefs about yourself, you will be attracting this higher frequency of energy towards you in the form of experiences and situations that confirm your positive beliefs and this is how you can achieve your heart's desires.

For those of you intrigued to learn more about this, in his book entitled *"The Biology of Belief"*, Dr Bruce Lipton explains in layman's terms the science behind this concept.

Gandhi explained it, more simply, like this,

Your beliefs become Your Thoughts

Your thoughts become Your Words

Your words become Your Actions

Your actions become your habits

Your habits become your values

Your values become your Destiny

I think one of the problems we have, and I have seen this in my clients, is not realising that we have these limiting subconscious beliefs in the first place. They are programmed into us at such an early age that we don't even know we have them, especially as some of our most limiting beliefs are actually taught to us in schools and society and from our parents, who we don't want to believe may have actually got stuff wrong.

For example, the self-fulfilling prophecy, as it is often referred to, where a child who is labelled a trouble maker will actually believe this of him or herself and become more of a trouble maker. Special needs children often go through the whole education system failing because they were led to believe early on that they couldn't do something or that they just weren't academic. So many teachers and parents, who don't understand how all this works are the ones responsible for programming such limiting beliefs. But it is us, ourselves, who reinforce these limiting beliefs as we get older, by believing what we've been told and not believing that we can easily change things. That is why it is so important to learn how to identify these beliefs that are, in effect, sabotaging our happiness.

Only then can we change them. This is, again, where we can refer to our list of affirmations. They are, in effect, a list of beliefs. You can read down the list and muscle test which ones you are not already congruent with and work on changing those.

Money is another subject that is really influenced by our subconscious limiting beliefs. If we have grown up in a household where money was tight we may have heard all sorts of *beliefs* such as;

Money is the root of all evil

You have to work hard if you want to make any money

Waste not want not

Money doesn't come easily

Save it for a rainy day

Don't spend it all at once

With these beliefs firmly programmed into our subconscious minds we will be emitting an energetic frequency of financial *lack* which will, in turn, bring us more financial *lack*.

So once we have identified these beliefs we need to reprogram our minds with new beliefs. We have seen the importance and role of affirmations in programming our subconscious minds but there are, in fact, other, quicker methods available to us. In the back of Dr Bruce Lipton's book, The Honeymoon Effect, he lists 27 belief changing modalities including The Body Code and PSYCH K®.

In addition to releasing trapped emotions and negative energy as we have already seen, The Body Code, by Dr Bradley Nelson, can also be used to release limiting subconscious beliefs which it refers to as Broadcast Messages and Despair Anchors.

It uses muscle testing to navigate the series of mind maps and, once a negative broadcast message has been identified, it can be released using the magnet and governing meridian line. (as with the trapped emotions mentioned earlier). In addition to this, new, healthy broadcast messages (or beliefs, affirmations ... whatever you want to call them) can be installed.

If you want to be able to do this yourself, you will need to invest in the Body Code program from Healer's Library. Again, I would recommend having a professional session first to learn more about it and see how you get on. Once you see how effective it is, you can purchase the programme and do it yourself. It will provide life changing healing for yourself and others you choose to work with.

In his book, The Honeymoon Effect, Dr Bruce Lipton openly rejoices in the healing both he and his wife, Margaret, have enjoyed with another modality called PSYCH K®. This motivated me to look into it further and qualify as a Practitioner.

PSYCH K®

PSYCH-K® increases the *cross-talk* between the two brain hemispheres, thus achieving a more *whole-brained* state. This is ideal for changing subconscious beliefs and facilitates communication with both the conscious and the subconscious minds to change old sabotaging belief patterns into supportive ones.

We have already seen how powerful the subconscious mind is, in as far as it makes up 90% of our mind with our conscious mind being the other 10%. The subconscious mind also accumulates and records information at over 40 million bits per second, storing memories in a timeless manner while the conscious part of our brain processes data at only 2000 bits per second and has a limited, 20-second memory capacity.

So if you have a subconscious belief that "*life is a struggle*" or that "*you'll never be rich*", it's generating at 40 million bits per second. The conscious mind, running at 2000 bits per second, usually cannot compete. It then creates conflict between the conscious and subconscious minds resulting in stress in the cells. This stress compromises the immune system and creates dis-ease in the body.

Through a series of specific balances, strategic body positioning, affirmations, and visualizations designed to bridge the right and left hemispheres of the brain, the self-limiting belief is re-scripted at the level of the subconscious until reprogramming is complete.

PSYCH-K® enables and empowers us to identify our limiting beliefs, change them by installing new healthy beliefs and therefore allows us to take control of whole areas of our lives. By changing your programming, you create the life you want, quickly, effortlessly and without the need for drugs, psychotherapy or a box of tissues.

Obviously I can't explain or describe the specific balances and body positioning here but it isn't dissimilar to the activities of Brain Gym already discussed in Chapter 1. It makes sense to me that by integrating the 2 halves of the brain, the new belief statement can be more easily absorbed and programmed into our subconscious minds especially if we set the intention of doing so.

"Whatever the mind of man can conceive and believe, it can achieve."
—Napoleon Hill

Chapter 6:
Raising Vibrations

"If you change the way you look at things, the things you look at change"
—Wayne Dyer

Levels of Consciousness

Being conscious is more than just being physically awake. To be conscious is to have awareness of one's thoughts, emotions, own existence, sensations, and surroundings.

Our consciousness can be compared to a lens through which we view and perceive the world. As we raise our consciousness we change the lens and our perceptions change causing a change in our reality. The perceptions, beliefs, mindsets and values we hold right now are a result of the consciousness we are operating in. Whenever we experience a shift in our consciousness due to an epiphany, an a-ha! moment or an inner realization, we are actually breaking away from our old consciousness and as a result, away from our old belief systems and attitudes.

Your thoughts, feelings, beliefs, values and actions reflect the level of consciousness that you are vibrating at. While the object you are observing, whether it be your life, world events, a person or a situation, can remain the same, just having a different consciousness level causes your thoughts, feelings, beliefs, values and actions to be widely different. This explains why different people can respond so differently to the same situations. If you *see* and *perceive* the situation to be different then your response to it will be different. For example, what do you see when faced with the playground bully? Do you see a nasty piece of work who needs to be taught a lesson by having a taste of his own medicine? Or do you see an angry and hurt child who is just crying out to be accepted and loved?

How do you view failure? Something to bring you down and shake your confidence? Or something to learn from and raise your motivation?

Dr David Hawkins (1913-2002) was a professor who, in his book Power vs Force (1995), created a Scale of Consciousness where he listed 17 different consciousness levels. For legal reasons I cannot include this chart here but I have taken some of the emotions he mentions and listed them below with their corresponding level of vibration. We have already seen that negative emotions vibrate at a lower level to positive emotions. We have also seen that we can improve our health by releasing these negative emotions. Here we can see that by continuing to raise our vibrations we can raise our consciousness and, by doing so, change our perceptions and realities.

Emotion	Level of Vibration
Enlightenment	700-1000
Peace	600
Joy	540
Love	500
Acceptance	350
Willingness	310
Neutrality	250
Anger	150
Fear	100

Guilt	30
Shame	20

Shame and Guilt are the lowest vibrating emotions followed by Fear. Fear is a big one. We find Fear in all areas of our life and our egos use fear to stop us from moving forwards. The emotion of Anger actually vibrates at quite a high level considering it's a negative emotion. This is because usually people who feel anger are *aware* of their emotion and it usually triggers a response. Maybe the response to anger won't be a positive one but acknowledging your feelings and responding is better than having apathy which vibrates at only 50.

If we look around us at the world today, and especially on the news, we can see many people stuck at the level of Anger although most of the planet are comfortably numb in their Neutrality vibrating at 250. According to Dr David Hawkins, personal survival is the main motivator up to this level, and for many who feel hopeless and depressed even personal survival may be lacking.

Above this level, motivation has greater meaning and at 500 love becomes the motivator. Sharing love and receiving joy in seeing others do well are characteristics. People excel creatively and demonstrate greater commitment and dedication at this level of consciousness. Their greater connection to Source energy and heightened intuition enable them to manifest their desires easily. At this level individuals can become inspirational leaders. The vision of such individuals can act to uplift society as a whole.

Dr David Hawkins continues by giving us some interesting figures. He says that the overall level of human consciousness tests as being just over 200, and only 4% of the population test over 500 and 1 in 10 million over 600.

He claims that just over 2% of the population generate 72% of society's problems. However, on the flip side, one individual at level 400 counterbalances 400,000 individuals vibrating below level 200, and one individual at 700 counterbalances 70 million below.

They say if you want to change the world you should begin by changing yourself. So it really is true and far more powerful than protesting or trying to directly change others. Even when faced with terrorism it's easy to harbour emotions of revenge, hatred and anger of course. But these emotions will just result in the lowering of your vibrations. They certainly won't help raise anyone else's. Yet, by responding with love and compassion we can see from the figures above, one person can achieve so much by raising the vibrations of so many.

By raising your own vibrations and consciousness level, you really will be counter balancing many others on a world scale. For me, this was an A ha moment and highlights exactly what we need to do, as in raise our vibrations, if we want to actively bring peace to this world.

The Healing Power of Forgiveness

"I forgive the past and set myself and others free"

When talking about how individuals vibrating at different consciousness levels perceive the world differently, we can see it most clearly in cases of revenge and forgiveness.

When we have been wronged or, more commonly, when our loved ones have been wronged or victimised it is very easy to feel anger, resentment and want to seek revenge. Forgiveness is often seen as a weakness. However, it is important to understand that

Forgiveness doesn't mean condoning the wrongful actions of others. It doesn't even have to involve communicating with the person who has wronged you. It relates to what's going on *inside* you and involves releasing the trapped negative emotions caused by this wrongdoing.

We saw earlier on Mark Twain's quote on anger and how it causes more damage to the person carrying it than to the person it's directed at. And we touched on the notion that some cancers are caused by trapped emotions of resentment. Well, when you can't forgive someone, what negative emotion are *you* hanging onto? Think about the damage it's doing to your health and the block to happiness that it is causing. Forgiveness is all about releasing us from the torment rather than being about the other person.

> *"Forgive others, not because they deserve forgiveness but because you deserve peace."*
> —Anon

Scarlett Lewis famously managed to find forgiveness for the gunman who ended her young son's life. So many would have let the anger, hurt, pain and resentment eat away at them and their health. The story of how she found forgiveness is documented in her book

Nurturing Healing Love: A Mother's Journey of Hope and Forgiveness.

I wanted to give Forgiveness its own subheading here. Not because there is so much to say about it but because of the important role it plays in our health and happiness. It is such an important area of our lives that we need to heal and it's not just the wilful wrongdoing of others that needs forgiveness. Most people harbour resentment and bitterness of some kind towards their parents for mistakes made during their childhood. Let's face it parenting isn't always easy and parents can only do their best with the knowledge and understanding that they have at the time.

It is also really important to note the healing power of forgiving *ourselves*. We are so good at beating ourselves up and making ourselves feel guilty about almost anything. Learning to forgive ourselves and releasing trapped emotions of guilt will raise your vibrations and help you heal.

Yoga

"I lovingly connect my mind, body and spirit"

"I lovingly move and exercise my body"

Yoga is thousands of years old and has its roots in spiritual traditions. The word yoga comes from the ancient Indian language of Sanskrit. It is a derivation of the word *yuj*, which means to yoke, as in joining a team of oxen, for example. It relates to the purpose of yoga being to join the mind, body, and spirit.

Yoga traditionally combines simple meditation, breath control and specific physical postures and is widely practised for health and relaxation.

One of the reasons that yoga is such a good activity is because it's very personal. There's no competition. Well, if there is, then you're doing it wrong! It's not about how far you can take each position. It's about focussing the mind on the present moment and helping that lovely, natural healing energy to flow around your body. Imagine it flowing to each part of you. Healing each body part and filling it with love. Yoga is a great opportunity to tell each part of you how much you love and appreciate it.

Yoga is also a great opportunity to lose yourself and your thoughts. It's also a good way to learn how to meditate. To put your conscious mind to the side for a while. Check what thoughts are subconsciously running through your head. These may well be negative subconscious beliefs you need to work on. Make a note of them and release them. Yoga is great for practicing to find that happy place inside of you. If all it does is bring up negatives then you know you've got some healing work to do. Yoga is the perfect time to repeat your affirmations. To run through your gratitude list. To identify the feelings that need to be released. Acknowledge how you feel while doing yoga. It really does open up our connection with source energy. It would be difficult to attend a decent yoga class and not feel heaps better in one way or another.

The beauty of going to an actual yoga class, is not only that you have a professional and knowledgeable teacher to work with but also that you have paid for that time to spend totally on yourself and yourself only. It's saying to the Universe, *"I am worth spending time on myself and I am willing to improve myself"*. However busy you are in life, once you have switched that phone off and trusted the teacher to tell you when the time is up, you are free to let it all go and concentrate 100% on *you*. This is clearly, also the case with any exercise class and I remember, in the past for me, finding exercise classes really quite emotional. I realise now it was because I hadn't learned to completely love myself and being left on my own, in my own head, was quite a vulnerable place for me to be at the time. If it feels like that to you, don't worry. It just means you have some inner work to do. By adopting the practical steps in this book with affirmations, gratitude and learning to love yourself, you'll soon feel more comfortable with being alone with yourself. After a bit more healing, you'll learn to love spending time on your own and in your own head! That's what it's all about!

If you can't get to a yoga class or it isn't your thing then don't worry. You can do some very simple yoga movements at home and there's lots of information for all levels on the internet. For the longest time I settled for doing yoga at home because I was on my own when my son was little and it was too impractical to attend a class. Now the important thing about doing any exercise and/or spiritual practice at home is not to beat yourself up. As you have probably realised by now, I am *not* a fan of people beating themselves up. If you make a strict program and tell yourself you've got to stick to it every day then for sure you'll conjure up all sorts of negative emotions like guilt, blame, resentment, frustration, failure ... the list goes on. We do not want these emotions trapped in us. We are trying to *raise* our vibrations, not *lower* them!

I knew if I told myself I had to follow an hour's yoga program, like many of the videos and DVDs, I would end up not doing it. So, as a sun lover, I simply took the Sun Salutation sequence in yoga and did that. The good thing about the Sun Salutation sequence is that it includes a number of positions that flow into each other and the full sequence varies from one instructor to the next. This was great because I could make it as basic or as complex as I liked. I started with an absolute basic sequence which you can easily find on the internet. Look at a few to see how they compare. Even a basic sequence will get you started with learning how to breathe at the correct times while moving and it uses most muscle groups which is great for getting that healing energy through your breath all around your body.

Ideally, I would suggest doing this first thing in the morning when no one else is up. The solitude is healing too in my opinion. You can do it in your pajamas or underwear so don't waste time wondering what to wear!

Now, because it is literally a 5 min routine you can't really shorten it so you'll more than likely achieve this. Already that will make you feel better. Do the same the next day, and the next. It's only 5 minutes. If you share your house, you could do it while waiting for the bathroom. Or waiting for the toast to do. Don't put any pressure on yourself. You will slowly learn to love it. You can then slowly and gradually add more poses to your routine. Add a lunge when you step backwards. Add a gentle back bend at the beginning and the end of the sequence.

You will find that your body naturally wants to add more to your morning routine. Mine did. And I can assure you that I am no expert in yoga. Just a fan. If you're having problems coordinating your breathing with the movement of the poses the *cat* is great. While kneeling on all fours simply breathe in as you arch your back upwards and breath out slowly as you arch your back downwards. Coordinating the breath with the movements gives your yoga routine greater impact and you will feel *even* better.

In fact, I kept adding bits to my routine and it ended up being 20 minutes long. Well, when you start with nothing this deserves a pat on the back. You can feel proud. Grateful. Energised. Happy. All those positive emotions. And you didn't have to beat yourself up. Just love yourself some more!

Meditation

*"The Soul always knows what to do to heal itself
The challenge is to silence the mind"*
—Caroline Myss

The word *meditation* probably has different meanings for different people and therefore gets interpreted in different ways.

According to Google's dictionary to meditate means:

to focus one's mind for a period of time, in silence or with the aid of chanting, for religious or spiritual purposes or as a method of relaxation.

I remember when I first heard about meditation, it was from a teaching colleague at a summer language school who was claiming that 20 minutes meditation gave him as much energy as sleeping for 8 hours. I was motivated to learn more about this as we were getting very little sleep what with having to say goodbye to departing students at the same time as welcoming arriving students throughout the night. Unfortunately, I didn't find meditation easy to learn.

The first thing is to quieten the mind. Easier said than done. Concentrating on your breathing helps. The mind wanders but rather than beating yourself up about it just gently bring your attention back to your breathing. It's important not to give up just because it's hard to clear your thoughts at first.

If it's difficult for you to clear your thoughts completely then try just keeping them to the present moment. This is an achievement in itself. If allowed to wander, the mind will usually worry about things in the future that haven't even happened yet or regret things from the past which we can't change anyway. Both are futile. Try and keep your thoughts in the present.

Guided meditations are great for beginners as you focus on the voice leading your thoughts. Guided meditations also get you into the practice of allowing yourself the time to meditate as well as finding the right peaceful place where you won't be disturbed. However, like spoon feeding a baby, it may be easy but it doesn't help the baby learn to feed itself. And when it does, it takes some practice before they can do it well. It's the same with meditation. Although there are numerous guided meditations available on the internet covering a wide range of issues and topics, they have not been designed for your unique body, mind and spirit. Only you will know what you need to achieve or focus on. With practice, holding that space for quiet contemplation gets easier. It becomes the perfect timeless moment and place to be in order to say our affirmations, offer our gratitude, raise our vibrations and heal our mind, body and spirit.

As you practice this further you can raise your level of consciousness and clearing your mind of all thoughts becomes easier. With practice you will find you can stay in the present moment. You will find you can connect more readily to source energy. This can be such a joyous feeling and a natural high. Try it and see.

Feng Shui

A dictionary definition of Feng Shui says,

"a system of laws considered to govern spatial arrangement and orientation in relation to the flow of energy (chi), and whose favourable or unfavourable effects are taken into account when siting and designing buildings."

Feng Shui is, basically, considering the natural, healthy flow of energy around buildings. As we are promoting the natural, healthy energy flow around our bodies, Feng Shui does the same for our houses and buildings. As with the energy within us, this energy flow around our buildings can get blocked and cause stagnant energy which in turn can cause unsettled feelings and negativity.

I first became aware of the effects and importance of Feng Shui, when my son was a toddler. We had cordoned off whole corners of the room to prevent him from touching things and causing harm, damage, a mess—or all three! We had a massive fire guard which took up half the living room. We had a play pen right in the middle of the room and there were stair gates to the kitchen, at the bottom of the stairs and at the top of the stairs. Everywhere was blocked but I hadn't noticed any of this until the day finally came when we could safely remove them all.

I remember feeling tremendous relief as the energy started flowing through the house once more. I could feel the energy literally *lift* and with it my mood immediately lightened. This led me to read a few books on the subject. The bit that stuck in my head the most was how negative it was to have your front door leading straight into a hallway which went straight up the stairs, which continued straight into the bathroom or worse still a toilet! Made worse if you just happened to have a roadway, or path coming straight towards your front door. That's exactly what we had at the time. A very typical and very British 2 up 2 down terraced house. Apparently, the energy would build up along the path (bringing all sorts with it!) go straight up our garden path, through our front door, along our hallway, up the stairs and down the toilet! Taking with it, apparently, any ounce of positive, healthy, prosperity energy with it. I was devastated! What could we do about the actual structure of our house? And what about all the other millions of people living in the UK with this typical style of house?

I got quite into it. The gate to the property had to be kept closed, as did the toilet seat! I didn't want all that healthy energy bound for me and my family to go straight down the loo! I read that wind chimes were an excellent way to break up any negative energy coming into the house so I quickly hung some in the hallway.

It's interesting to read some of the other aspects of Feng Shui as well. Mirrors are very important. Put one over the family dining table. It will reflect the food on the table and encourage the continuation of plentiful amounts of food for the family. But don't have mirrors in the bedroom, well not reflecting the bed, especially if you are a couple. It will reflect and add people to your bed, apparently encouraging extra marital affairs and relationship troubles.

Feng Shui can also affect your finances and your health. You'll need a compass to work out the orientation of each corner of your house. Your bed should face a certain direction for optimum benefit and plants and water features are important too. Arrows and points are not good and neither are spiky plants. I'm no expert, as I'm sure you can tell by now, but there's definitely something in this.

In my last house, which was built on a mountain and had different levels, there were some ugly looking railings with sharp spikes pointing down to the neighbour's garden. I initially wanted them removed but they were there to prevent anyone, namely burglars, from climbing round to the balcony door so I kept them. However, it was very noticeable that the trees directly in line with those arrows were all dead or dying. Arrows and spikes direct negative energy to where they are pointing. There was no other apparent reason for this. The other trees in the garden were all flourishing.

Now I am much more sensitive to energy and I can feel a negative build up in the corners of rooms especially where loads of electricity cables are present like behind the TV. Clapping in the corners really helps with this. I am fully aware of how silly this sounds but clapping, or ringing a bell, in the corners of rooms can really lift and circulate stale energy. I used to do this every time I started in a new classroom in my school teaching days. It made such a difference. Before you laugh too loudly, why not try it in your own home and feel the difference!

Diet and Exercise

"I lovingly feed my body nourishing foods and beverages"

You must be both surprised and relieved to see that a book about healing and health has such a small section on Diet and Exercise. You are probably expecting to read all sorts of advice on what to eat and what not to eat. Advice on portion size and how to avoid all the foods you love. Or maybe you're expecting me to scare you with shock tactics? People promoting diet and exercise often use mind games to make you feel guilty and they encourage the concept of will power.

Well, you'll be pleased to hear I don't believe in that approach. In fact, I firmly believe that it can do more harm than good. Why would you want to add more guilt to your body when we have been focussing on releasing such negative emotions? If you set yourself an unachievable fitness regime, you're setting yourself up to feel failure when your body doesn't want to stick to it. Another negative emotion.

No, as far as I'm concerned it's all about *love*. Loving yourself. And listening to yourself. Listening to the *you* inside.

"I am willing to change the way I think about food"

When it comes to raising our vibrations food is an easy way to do so. Foods, as we have already seen, are just energy, like everything else. And they all vibrate at different frequencies. Organic food is high vibrational food as opposed to processed foods where you can't even tell what's in it. I always like to *see* what I'm eating. I like to see what's going into what I'm eating. If you have to read a tiny label on a packet to know what you're putting into your mouth, I'd rather not eat it. You should be able to *recognise* your food and the ingredients that went into it!

My advice is to go back to basics. Eat from the land. I know it's hard in the cities these days, especially with all the GMOs etc but if organic produce has found its way to me in my tiny Spanish village then you should be able to find some healthier options if you look. And please don't use money as an excuse. There is no price on health and happiness.

I am not a fan of diets. As I have said, listen to your body's own advice and not that of someone else who doesn't know you. But having said that, the Paleo Diet seems to be very popular at the moment which, according to its definition on Google, appears to carry sound advice,

"a diet based on the types of foods presumed to have been eaten by early humans, consisting chiefly of meat, fish, vegetables, and fruit and excluding dairy or cereal products and processed food."

Either way, healthier foods have higher vibrating energy than unhealthy foods. This is not rocket science. We all feel sluggish and tired after eating the wrong foods for our bodies or after eating too much food however much we *think* we like it at the time.

And *thinking* that we like something is a relevant point here. We have already seen that we can develop addictions to foods that we are most intolerant to. Addiction is an emotional attachment. We create our addictions from an emotional need. It's the same with over-eating (or under-eating) or comfort eating as it is so commonly referred to. The scenario where the jilted partner reaches for the ice cream is a classic case.

We use food in an attempt to fill an emotional void. If it works, it does so only in the short term. Often, especially after over-eating, we actually feel worse, because we have added guilt, failure and even self hate to the equation. All that when really all you needed was love. Love is all you need. Sorry to sound like a Beatles song here, but they had a point! Wouldn't it be easier to just add the love that your body really craves?

We often turn to the fridge to satisfy our emotional hunger as well as our physical hunger and the problem being, we often can't differentiate the two. Here's a couple of tips to test if you're really physically hungry or not. Firstly, drink a large glass of water. Never underestimate the importance of drinking plenty of water. Some bodies confuse thirst for hunger. If you still feel hungry, try a couple of rounds of EFT. You know how now. *"Even though I feel hungry"*, karate chop, *"I love and accept myself completely"*. Go.

If you still feel hungry then you probably are so get yourself a sensible, light meal. If not, continue with the tapping to release whatever emotions you have inside causing you to feel hunger.

Once you have released the negative emotions, added the love and raised your vibrations, your body will tell you what it wants by giving you mini healthy cravings. You will feel so much better after eating. It will even make you *want* to exercise!

Our bodies naturally want to stretch their legs after a long car journey. Or we feel the need to go for a walk when we've been cooped up all day. Desk workers naturally stretch backwards and stretch their arms out when their bodies need it. It's the same with exercise. Just listen to your body. It will tell you when it needs to move. Find something that interests you. Find something that's fun. It doesn't have to be an exercise class or an organised sport. Bowling with friends. Walking along the seafront. Fruit picking. Scuba diving. Trampolining. Now I have never seen anyone sad on a trampoline! The important thing is that you *enjoy* what you do.

"Do the Thing that Makes your Heart Sing!"

Pets and Nature

Pets are great for a number of reasons. Giving love helps us receive love especially when it's unconditional love. They actually help us learn to love ourselves. They give us the opportunity to see the good in ourselves and we can nurture that feeling as we nurture them.

Pets are also very calming. Stroking them is relaxing. They learn to love us and we benefit from that energy. They also, well I guess dogs mainly, need walking and this is great because we do too! They give us an excuse to go to the beach and play. They encourage us to get into nature. Like children. It can be so uplifting to spend time in the woods, park, beach, mountains, fields, wherever.

Take your shoes off when you get there. Connect with the earth. Breathe. The great outdoors. Bring it in. This is why so many guided meditations involve imagining yourself in a beautiful countryside setting. If you do live miles from the countryside or beach then get plenty of plants. Nurture them and you will see, in turn they will nurture you.

Essential Oils

Here is an easy way to boost your energy and raise your vibrations and you don't have to be an expert in any of these to benefit from them.

Well having said that you shouldn't actually *blend* essential oils unless you are a qualified Aromatherapist. Oils can be very powerful but the only one to really avoid, and that's only if you are early days pregnant, is clary sage. It is great for helping the flow, so to speak, of menstrual periods and menopause. It helps the flow emotionally and physically which is why it is not recommended for pregnant women. However, you will find that if you need an oil for healing you will be drawn to that oil. When training as an Aromatherapist, I couldn't work out how one day I would love the smell of clarey sage and the following week I'd find it almost repulsive. It was only when I learned of its properties that I realised. We are naturally drawn to what we need.

Lavender oil is a natural sedative and it helps you sleep well and calms you. If you need to relax, burning some lavender oil (2 drops in water using a typical oil burner with a tea light beneath) will help greatly. It works so well at aiding sleep I wouldn't recommend it if you have things to do. A couple (but no more) of drops on your pillow at night will ensure a good night's sleep.

Here are some more of my favourites.

Black pepper is great for keeping warm as it works on the circulation system.

Ylang ylang is the best aphrodisiac!

Grapefruit is a natural anti-depressant. Use this if you're feeling down. It will immediately lift your spirits.

Frankincense is luxurious and makes you feel it!

Rosemary is great if you need mental clarity. I have a Rosemary bush outside my office and regularly pick a sprig when I need to focus and concentrate the mind.

Adding drops to your bath is also a great way to unwind and benefit from these oils.

You should never use oils neat especially on the body. For massage always mix a couple of drops with a carrier oil such as grape seed oil.

Admittedly, I've picked my favourites here. If you could smell the oils you should go with whatever you're drawn to because, as we've already mentioned, you will be drawn to the ones you need the most. But for now, this was just some quick tips to help you sleep, focus and raise your vibrations.

Crystals and Colour

Both crystals and colour are an easy and effective way to boost your energy and raise your vibrations. They are both such extensive topics, I can't possibly cover everything here so I will just mention some of my favourite tips.

A big lump of black tourmaline by the front door will help absorb negative energy. They are self cleansing which makes them very practical. Small pieces of black tourmaline are great for carrying in your pocket when faced with negative people or a negative environment at work for example.

Amethysts are, in my opinion, the best all rounders. They are the lavender of the crystal world. Placed under your pillow they will aid sleep and they are great for opening up your awareness to your Higher Self.

A rose quartz in the bra can help settle a troubled relationship and a turquoise is great to wear if you need help with speaking up about something or you have a presentation or other speaking engagement. It can also help in times when you need to listen more intently.

If any of this is resonating with you then you will be guided to explore the wonderful world of crystals and how to look after them.

For those of you who don't know the Chakras and their associated crystals and colours I've drawn up this simple chart.

Chakras are our energy centres within the body, each relating to a different body part and aspect of our health. They become imbalanced when we need healing in a particular area of our body or area of our life. There are many ways in which we can balance our Chakras, one being The Emotion Code which we have already looked at, but we can also help balance them by wearing crystals and colours related to the imbalanced Chakra.

Chakra	Chakra Name	Body Part	Area of Life	Colour	Crystal Suggestions
First	Root/Base	Base of the spine	groundedness stability, belonging, basic trust	Red, brown, earthy, black	red jasper, hematite, black tourmaline, black obsidian
Second	Sacral	Below the navel, Reproductive organs/bladder	sexuality, creativity, family, lovers, fruitfulness	Orange	carnelian, orange calcite
Third	Solar Plexus	Between navel and breastbone	power, wisdom, confidence, strength	Yellow	citrine
Fourth	Heart	Heart, centre of the chest	love, joy, matters of the heart, healing	Green and Pink	green aventurine, malachite, rose quartz
Fifth	Throat	Throat, neck	communication, expression	Blue	turquoise, angelite, sodalite
Sixth	Third Eye	Just above the centre of the eyebrows	Intuition, insight, vision, awareness	Dark blue, indigo	lapis lazuli, azulite
Seventh	Crown	The crown of the head and just above it	Connection with source energy, spirituality	Violet, golden white	amethyst

When buying crystals you can usually find Chakra sets which will include crystals for each Chakra. Wearing them on your person in the right place really helps. You'll need pockets! Or a bra! Wearing crystals, especially the heart chakra ones, is easy to do in a bra if you wear one! Or a top pocket if you don't! Clothes of the right colour can also help. Orange knickers are great for helping to balance the Sacral chakra. Blue scarves will help protect and balance your throat chakra. Yellow, green or pink shirts all help with these chakras.

Colour therapy is often something we do subconsciously. Have you ever stood in front of your open wardrobe and been drawn to an item of clothing without knowing why? As we have seen, we are naturally drawn to the healing we need. People newly in love wear a lot of green as an expression of their overflowing heart chakra. On the flipside I have also seen people newly heartbroken wear a lot of green as they are subconsciously reaching out for help with healing their broken heart. Orange is great if you're looking for the right lover or if you are looking to be fruitful whether literally by getting pregnant or metaphorically with your career. Confident people and indeed people needing a confidence boost will be drawn to yellow. Unfortunately yellow is a difficult colour for many to wear. Well, for me it is. I have a selection of large coloured scarves and when I need a particular healing boost I wrap myself up in whichever colour is right at night. This is a good way to benefit from yellow and boost your confidence without actually wearing it! I do remember once, when on an unpleasant flight, holding my son's yellow teddy bear to my solar plexus to strengthen my power centre. You may well laugh but it worked!

So as far as colour goes, my advice to help you heal yourself, is to invest in a range of large coloured scarves as well as crystals. Still your mind, breathe deeply, relax and see which one you're drawn to. And wear it. Even if it's just in bed at night!

When you're naturally drawn to purple, it's a sign that you are well on the way to spiritual awakening! What colours are you drawn to?

Music

We saw in Chapter 2, with Masaru Emoto's water crystals, how music played an important role in beautifying water molecules. Heavy metal sounds made the water molecules irregular, disjointed and basically ugly in nature. Whereas playing John Lennon's Imagine to water samples resulted in the water crystals becoming balanced, regular and pretty in comparison. To be honest, who doesn't feel love when listening to the song *Imagine*?

Music is also great, of course, because it can make us want to move and dance and fills us literally with Good Vibrations.

For those of you who are more musically orientated you can check out Sound Therapy. Sound is very healing. There are particular notes that relate to each chakra too. Again, it's an extensive topic and one I can't cover here but maybe something here will trigger something within you to learn more.

"If music be the food of love, play on."
—William Shakespeare, Twelfth Night

Making Love

Needless to say, making love is an excellent way to raise your vibrations. Having said that though, having sex with the wrong person can be a major cause of trapping negative emotions i.e. guilt, shame, unworthiness, trauma. Please be discerning when it comes to choosing your sexual partners. I realise that some of you may not have met your perfect partner yet, in which case the next chapter is for you.

Chapter 7:
Attracting Love

"I am loving, lovable and loved"

Love is misunderstood to be an emotion; actually, it is a state of awareness, a way of being in the world, a way of seeing oneself and others."
—*David R. Hawkins*

Love vs Fear

Some say there are just 2 emotions in life. Love and Fear. And like darkness is just the absence of light, Fear is just the absence of Love.

Fear isn't just about being scared of something. It is the emotion of the ego, used to try and control us into not changing or growing.

The more Love you can put into your body, the less fear you will have.

Changing from an outlook based on fear to one of pure love is not always easy especially in today's world with the bias, politics and terrorism that fill our media. During these turbulent times there appears to be a greater polarity than ever before between the two major energetic forces of Love and Fear.

This is not about Good vs Evil. We cannot control the evil of others. This is about our *response* to it. A response of fear is not only giving our power away, but it also creates more fear and perpetuates negative situations.

Fear is a powerful motivational tool exploited by just about anyone who thinks they can profit from it. And I don't just mean the politicians, advertisers, media, and religious leaders. I am also referring to some employers, the legal system and the many people in abusive relationships to name a few examples. All controlled by fear. Even on a lighter note, fear holds us back from making positive moves in life. Fear of failure may stop an entrepreneur starting out. People staying in stale relationships feel fear of being alone and, without faith, there is always fear of the unknown. Fear of not making enough money. I am always coming across people who use money, or rather the lack of it, as a cover for their fear of change and the unknown.

"So many of us choose our path out of fear
disguised as practicality"
—Jim Carrey

Fortunately, love is an even more powerful motivating force, but can often be overshadowed by fear. Fear seems to spread more readily, it's louder, harsher and used by so many in supposed authority.

So what happens to your energetic field as you pick up and absorb the energy around you? Are you looking at life from a fear perspective? Do you regularly get caught up in worry and self-doubt? Or do you see love all around you and live intuitively from your heart?

Fear, of course, is a natural primal response to threats of survival and can serve us well. However, the fear that holds us back most in life is the fear of failure, the fear of rejection and the fear of the unknown as in moving out of our comfort zones.

"There are two basic motivating forces: fear and love. When we are afraid, we pull back from life. When we are in love, we open to all that life has to offer with passion, excitement, and acceptance. We need to learn to love ourselves first, in all our glory and our imperfections. If we cannot love ourselves, we

cannot fully open to our ability to love others or our potential to create. Evolution and all hopes for a better world rest in the fearlessness and open-hearted vision of people who embrace life."
—John Lennon

People who have experienced great fear in their lives often hold onto it as a trapped emotion. It's the *Once bitten twice shy* syndrome again. If you have been badly bitten by a dog, for example, you may well feel fear of all dogs long after the event. Every time you see a dog you will add to that fear until it becomes an irrational phobia. Fortunately, as we saw in Chapter 3 with The Emotion Code and EFT, you can heal yourself of this problem by releasing the trapped emotions of fear. Fear, when allowed to grow like this, can be a debilitating state of mind that weakens body and soul, and can be associated with heart conditions, nervous disorders, stress, depression, phobias and paranoia.

Fear also makes us act selfishly with no concern for others. Think about when you were last fearful. How did you react? How did your fear impact those around you? Whereas love encompasses all those around us and radiates compassion. Think of your last display of love, how did it impact those around you?

Loving Your Inner Child

Much of the pain we suffer today is a result of how we were treated as a child. As children we are not mature enough or aware enough to reason with the negative experiences we are faced with and we haven't yet learned to see the limitations of the people, namely parents, who are causing us the upset. As adults we can understand that the bully is hurting too. A victim of their own perceptions. Our parents too, unwillingly, pass their perceptions and pain onto us. Our vulnerability in childhood can lead even simple everyday events to leave their mark on us. Angry parents. Raised voices. Distracted parents. Busy parents. Money conscious parents. Unfair parents. Sibling favouritism. Upset parents. Hurting parents. Forgetful parents.

The expression *From the Cradle to the Grave* can be so true. What we are told as infants will stay with us till we die. Unless, of course, we acknowledge it and change it. The power is within us all to do so.

Inner child work is an excellent way to heal old hurts from childhood, however serious or not they may be. Hypnotherapists typically use this method in their regression work and coaches and other therapists use it to heal old wounds. You can, of course, do it yourself.

While lying down somewhere comfortable and alone, quietly and calmly relax your body. Close your eyes and breathe deeply. Give yourself some time. Think about your childhood. What events come to mind? Can you remember an incident where you felt hurt? Can you remember an event where a parent upset you?

Picture yourself as that child at that time. Visualise where you were. What you were wearing. How you were feeling. In your mind go up to that child now as the adult you are today and give them a hug. Tell them how much you love them. Tell them how special they are. What did you want to hear from your parent, or other person causing the pain at the time? Imagine the words you wanted to hear at the time. Imagine the comfort you wished you'd had at the time. Now as the adult you are today, give that comfort to your inner child self. Say the words you wanted to hear. Reassure your inner child. Hold your inner child. Love your inner child. Tell your inner child all the things you wanted to hear.

Stay in this embrace as you feel the intensity of the pain fade away. Crying is good. Stay. In your mind. Visualising. Comforting. Holding. Loving.

When the tears and pain have subsided let go. Ask your inner child how they feel now. You may need to repeat the process. It may bring up other such events. Keep going. Your body and your inner child will guide you. As you leave this meditation process, imagine your parent or whoever it was who had, wittingly or unwittingly caused you pain, and Forgive them. Clearly and openly tell them you understand their pain, their problems at the time and Forgive them. Tell them they are forgiven. Lie there and absorb this powerful healing for a while longer. As you slowly come back to the now, how do you feel?

You don't need to forgive this person in real life. Send them love. Send them lots of love. Remember to send yourself heaps too!

If you are not ready to do this for yourself yet, seek professional help. It is by adding love that we can release pain and fear. This is how we can heal. This is what will bring greater happiness.

Finding Mr/Mrs Right

Finding Mr or Mrs Right is something we all want to manifest. That blissful state of not only being in love but of staying in love that eludes so many. Maybe some of you will have got quite sceptical about it and maybe you have chosen to believe that your perfect partner doesn't exist but this is not the case. If you think there is no Mr or Mrs Right for you out there it's purely because *you* are not out there for them yet. You are not ready to receive them into your life yet.

We know that *like* attracts *like*. So, if you have "issues" holding you back from happiness then you will attract relationships with people who also have "issues" holding them back from their happiness.

If you have trapped emotions and beliefs of guilt, shame, anger, worthlessness etc. you will be a perfect vibrational match for someone else also full of those negative, trapped emotions and beliefs. So in fact, if you have been attracting the "wrong" kind of guy or girl into your life, you can understand why. You are attracting the "like".

You are attracting people with the same vibrations as you. With the same issues as you. Now this doesn't have to be a reason for the relationship to fail but with all those negative emotions and issues coming to the fore it could be a turbulent ride. But if both parties are prepared to work on improving themselves individually within the relationship then of course there's success at hand. The important point here is that you are not responsible for each other's happiness. Our happiness can only come from within ourselves. And if we rely on someone else to make us happy we are giving away our power.

Equally, other people can only make us feel bad if we let them. If we give them the power to do so. Obviously, we can support each other. Give unconditional love to each other but we are not responsible for their happiness just as they are not responsible for ours.

Remember, you will have to put up with whatever it is you choose to accept in a relationship. If you allow someone to treat you badly then they will and you will have to put up with that. If you don't want to put up with certain behaviours in your relationship then don't accept it. This is hard for many I know. But if you begin to accept unwanted behaviour you will get unwanted behaviour. So set your boundaries and stick to them. Making yourself unhappy isn't going to create the perfect relationship is it?

So unless you are prepared to work together on this self development process you are best parting company while working on healing yourself first. If the relationship is meant to be then it will be. Your aim is to raise your vibrations and learn to love yourself. As I said before, if you can't love yourself, how can you expect someone else to love you? And if you can't love yourself how can you truly love another person?

Once you have learned to love yourself, released some of the fear causing your issues and raised your vibrations you will be a magnet for partners who match that vibration.

So basically if you want to meet Mr or Mrs Right, you need to first be that Mr or Mrs Right to be a vibrational match. The higher your vibrations the higher their vibrations will be. Therefore, if you don't want to attract someone with "issues" then sort yours out first!

There is nothing like a close, intimate relationship to highlight all our flaws. With someone literally witnessing your life it will be hard to ignore any areas you need to develop. To give the relationship the best possible chance and yourself the best opportunity to heal you will need to face these flaws when they arise. Acknowledge them and take responsibility for them and, hopefully, with open and compassionate communication, your partner can support you while you resolve any issues as you support them to do the same in return. Strong relationships where both parties can heal, grow and develop on a personal level are not usually forged easily but rather take a lot of courage, commitment and soul searching. However, they are also rewarding for exactly those reasons. Admitting our issues instead of hiding them or denying them is a start. If you think about it, it is often our attempts to hide our flaws and our eagerness to apportion blame that lead to instability in our relationships. Accepting responsibility for our flaws and being willing to grow will have a more favourable outcome all round.

Remember, guilt, shame and blame are all low vibrating emotions which will keep you in a state of attracting more of the same. By exercising acceptance, compassion, willingness and love you will receive these positive qualities in return. That is a much healthier and happier place to be, don't you agree?

Chapter 8:
Attracting Prosperity

"I welcome Prosperity into my life"

Are You Focusing on Lack?

Remember that *Energy flows where our Attention Goes*. In other words, we will get what we think about. We manifest what we focus on. In Chapter 1 we looked at how to word our affirmations. *"I am clearing my debts"* or *"I am debt free"* is not a good affirmation because it directs our thoughts to those of *debt*.

However, even if we focus on *money* as opposed to *debt* there can still be problems. It will depend on what the word money means to you and how it makes you feel.

When you think about the word money, how do you feel? Money can be such an emotionally fuelled word. The meaning of the word will differ from person to person but we all grow up with a relationship to money. And to most of us it was seen as something that controlled us and the things we did.

I was brought up with the phrase *Waste Not Want Not* and still to this day I find it hard to throw unwanted food and other items away or to buy a more expensive product as opposed to settling for the cheapest.

How does the word money, and the meaning you have put on it, make you feel?

Does money conjure up feelings of Resentment? Self worth? Anger even? or Failure? Despair? Or does it make you feel joyous, relaxed and comfortable?

Money is just a word. We know that words, our thoughts about them and the meaning we give to them are just energy.

There is no point in saying an affirmation about money if the word money is going to direct your thoughts to your lack of money or your resentment of money. If you have developed a dislike of money or even a hatred then that energy that you are feeling about money will act as a deterrent and keep money away from you. You will be energetically keeping money from coming to you because you are feeling that negative energy about it.

This is why, as I said in Chapter 1, using the words prosperity and abundance is a better option. And here is a good opportunity to point out the importance of following all these practical steps together because having gratitude for what you've already got is a sure fire way of receiving more.

It would feel wrong to affirm that you have plenty of money when your bank balance clearly shows the opposite. But you can affirm your abundance and prosperity. You have food to eat, right? A roof over your head? Friends and family? Clothes? A computer or other device, right? Start giving gratitude for and affirming the abundance and prosperity you already have. The Universe will respond and bring you more. Do this and you'll see.

Money vs Prosperity

Another reason to focus on your prosperity rather than on money itself is because there is a difference between the two. They may be linked but there is a big difference between them.

When affirming that money is coming our way or that our income is increasing we are focussing on *money* basically. Which isn't a bad thing if you have positive thoughts about money but so many people have negative belief patterns about the subject of money. Prosperity, on the other hand, is more than just money and prosperity can come to us in more ways than money can.

This is also where I want to remind you that we shouldn't focus on how these things are going to come to us. That would only limit and possibly hinder it getting to us. If we think about the different ways we can increase our bank balance for sure these ways will be small in number compared to the ways the Universe can find to bring them to us.

Many people, I know, are in the situation that I was in where they have a "day job" and do the thing they love as a hobby or part time job whether it be writing, working with animals, energy healing or whatever. It is their part time job that uses their divine creativity and it's where their heart truly lies. Envisaging this activity as being able to support them completely is often a stumbling block to their manifestations.

I adopted this following affirmation:

"I allow myself to be fully financially supported

Doing work that is aligned with my highest values and greatest dreams,

Opportunities to share my gifts and skills

come to me in expected and unexpected ways,

I let go of the "hows" and let the Universe help me

I am a magnet for miracles

And so it is"

When you focus on the outcome of *prosperity* and not *money* and you don't focus on *how* this prosperity will come, you open up so many more pathways for the Universe to provide it for you. In my case, by a divine turn of events and timing, my expenses halved. At the time, it wasn't a case of more money coming in but, with half the expenses, I had, in effect, more money!

That's prosperity. I had been affirming *"I allow myself to be fully financially supported doing work that is aligned with my highest values and greatest dreams"* and there I was. Another affirmation had come true. But not by increasing my income. By halving my expenses. I was more prosperous. That's how money and prosperity differ. Focus on your prosperity and you will get more prosperity. Don't think about how. And when it comes, be grateful, very grateful for it.

Chapter 9:
Our Thoughts Create Our Reality

"Thoughts become Things so Choose the Best Ones"
—Mike Dooley

The Placebo Effect

"The power of our beliefs can work in either direction to become life-affirming or life-denying"
—Gregg Braden

In 1955, a man called Beecher, an anaesthetist in Boston, published a paper entitled "The Powerful Placebo." In it, he described his research of more than two dozen medical case histories. His findings, documented that up to one-third of the patients healed from their conditions by taking "pretend" medication. That is to say, by taking a course of treatment that had no known healing agents. The term used to describe this phenomenon is commonly known as the placebo effect.

During the testing of the Placebo Effect, the placebo used ranged from a sugar pill or saline solution to actual surgery where nothing was actually done. Some patients, willing to participate, actually underwent all of the experiences of surgery, including anaesthesia, incisions, and sutures, while in reality nothing is added, taken away, or changed. No organs were treated. No tumours were removed. As someone who believes that surgery seriously imbalances the body's natural energy field and should, therefore, always be considered as a last resort to any healing, this makes me cringe. Although it did prove a very important point.

That point being that the patients believed something was being done. Based on their trust of the doctor and modern medicine, they believed that what they had experienced would help their condition. In the presence of their belief, their body responded as if they had actually taken the drug or undergone a real procedure.

Other studies have recorded an even higher response rate, depending on the condition for which patients were treated.

The following excerpt from an article published in The New York Times in 2000 reveals just how powerful the placebo effect can be,

"Forty years ago, a young Seattle cardiologist named Leonard Cobb conducted a unique trial of a procedure then commonly used for angina, in which doctors made small incisions in the chest and tied knots in two arteries to try to increase blood flow to the heart. It was a popular technique with 90 percent of patients reporting that it helped but when Cobb compared it with placebo surgery in which he made incisions but did not tie off the arteries, the sham operations proved just as successful. The procedure, known as internal mammary ligation, was soon abandoned."

There are plenty of other examples of research and findings that I could include here but you've got the idea. Some of them even refer to the doctor's concern and caring attitude as being a primary factor in the success rates of the placebo.

If life-affirming beliefs do in fact have the power to reverse disease and heal our bodies, then we must ask ourselves an obvious question. How much damage do negative beliefs create?

Dr Bruce Lipton often uses Angelina Jolie as an example of this. Having lost a number of family members to breast cancer, she was reportedly given a 70% chance of also getting it. She decided to have a double mastectomy to avoid this. Later, she learned of having a 50% chance of getting ovarian cancer so had her ovaries removed too. We will never know what could have happened had she focussed her thoughts and beliefs on being among the 50% that wasn't going to get it.

"Thoughts Create our Reality.

Your Thoughts create Your reality.

When you think of something

your subconscious takes note.

The more you focus on that thought,

the more memories you create,

the more emotions you feel while you focus,

the more powerful these memories.

Your subconscious learns how important these thoughts are

and takes note.

Your super conscious notices these memories

and

without judging

slowly but surely,

if you let it happen,

these thoughts will manifest into your reality every time"
—Abraham Hicks

Energy Flows Where Attention Goes

"The moment you change your perception is the moment you re-write the chemistry of your body."
—Bruce Lipton

Remember, with wanting to clear debts we must focus on our prosperity and not our debt. Well it's the same with many things. The phrase Anti-War still mentions the word War and that, in itself, will trigger thoughts and ideas around our bodies. We will *think* war and unwittingly create *more* energy related to war. It's the same with the word Cancer. Anti Cancer charities are not doing themselves any favours by focussing everyone's attention on the word Cancer. Especially when these words are so emotionally charged. We all end up *thinking* about the very thing we want to avoid. This is where I applaud the Race for Life. This is how to raise awareness. Focus on what you want i.e. life and not what you don't want i.e. cancer. Be Pro Peace not Anti War.

Our thoughts will ultimately create our reality whether we like it or not. Whether we believe it or not. Negative thoughts will and do create negative experiences. This is why it is so important to check your thoughts and make a note of how you are thinking. What are you expecting? How are you feeling? Shifting your perceptions and beliefs and thinking positively is so important for your health and happiness.

If you think the world is a loving place, full of friendly people and positive life experiences you will feel and benefit from that supportive energy. On the other hand, if you think the world is a hostile place and full of negativity, then, for you, it will be. It's your choice.

"The most important decision we make is whether we believe we live in a friendly or hostile universe."
—Albert Einstein

The Law of Attraction

"Everything is energy and that's all there is to it. Match the frequency of the reality you want and you cannot help but get that reality. It can be no other way. This is not philosophy. This is physics."
—Albert Einstein

Some call it *The Secret* after the famous book, which, if you haven't read yet, I strongly urge you to, or indeed watch the film of the same name. Although, to be honest it's basically saying what I've already said in this book. I hope I'm not getting too repetitive here but simply put, you need to raise your vibrations to exactly match those of the experience or thing you are wanting and that's it! The rest is not a secret. It's science!

Imagine that you already have what you want and think about how much you love having it. Think about how grateful you are to have whatever it is. Remember the bit about being grateful for what prosperity you already have? Well, it's all the same.

"Appreciation in advance brings everything you want to you"
—Abraham Hicks

Now when it comes to the Law of Attraction there are many great names who mention it but the best teacher is Abraham, if you're ready to accept and digest their advice. I say *their* because Abraham is actually a *"group consciousness from the non physical dimension"*. Their words come to us via Esther Hicks. Now if this is already too much for your sceptical mind then leave this bit and come back to it later when you feel ready. Focus on the factual science behind attracting the same energy that you give out. For those of you, on the other hand, open to the truth I urge you to read or listen to the teaching of Abraham Hicks as it provides the best explanation of the Law of Attraction.

Louise Hay calls them, *"some of the best teachers on the planet today."*

Dr. Wayne Dyer said they are, *"the great Masters of the Universe!"*

In April 2007, on the Abraham Mexican Well-Being Cruise, Abraham explained who "they" are in this way,

"We are as broad or as deep as the question that you ask because Law of Attraction will not match you up with the part of us which is different from the part of you,

We can only be as wise as your wisdom, as loving as your love and as smart as your brilliance,

We cannot be more than you allow us to be so when you find something in us that you deem worthy or wonderful or beneficial you must understand that it is a pure reflection of who you are because you could not get it from us if you were not it also."

So, how exactly can we use the Law of Attraction to manifest our heart's desires? I'm going to attempt to explain how very simply.

So firstly you have to set your intention. What do you want? What is your desire? Remember the advice from the affirmations. Keep it positive and keep it vague. Don't desire *how* you are going to get it. Just set the end result of having it. Don't limit yourself. It doesn't matter if *you* can't see how it will come. *How* it comes is not your department. Set an affirmation in place. And write a note for your Reiki box or Dream Board.

Then you are going to visualise having it. Smell it, feel it, taste it, see it, touch it. Imagine you already have it. How do you feel about having this desired object or thing? Feel gratitude for having it.

Now for the difficult bit. Step back from the outcome. Hand over your desire to whoever resonates with you. Angels, Source Energy, God, Creator, Higher Self, whoever. But you *do* have to take what we call action steps. In addition to the affirmations and gratitude in advance you have to read the right stuff, or eat the right food, or apply for the right jobs, or look for the right car, or meet new people or whatever is relevant to your desire. You can't sit on the sofa all day and do nothing.

Some of the action steps you take will come to nothing. In fact, many of them will but that doesn't matter. You have to be willing to do something. You won't meet Mr or Mrs Right while watching TV in your front room. You can't get your dream job if you haven't applied for any. You won't lose weight if you stuff yourself with cream doughnuts! Put yourself in the right place to achieve what it is you desire.

Then comes the faith. Keep the faith. If you let thoughts of "It won't work" sneak in then it won't work. Don't give up and definitely don't focus on how your desire will come about. You just have no idea what The Universe is kicking into motion behind the scenes on your behalf. Your mind won't be able to fathom the infinite possibilities that can come in to force now. Separate yourself from all that curiosity.

I once read a really cool analogy about this using the metaphor of a car and the sat nav (GPS). I'm afraid I can't remember where or by whom so please let me know who originally said it, if you know.

When sitting in your car, if you have the gearstick in Park you are not going to go anywhere and you won't achieve anything. You need to put your car into Drive.

Then you tap your destination (desire) into the sat nav. Now, it can take you along many routes but you just want the quickest one, right? So you Trust your sat nav to provide you with the quickest route. You don't ask it how, you just trust it.

Now you have to take action. You have to start the ignition. You have to move forwards. Slowly at first. You have to signal and use mirrors and take lots of other action steps to get to your destination. You may come across some road blocks or traffic jams. You stay patient and enjoy the journey. You still have faith that you're going in the right direction despite a delay or two.

Now you may well go down a wrong road. Some sat navs are a little out of date, right? You don't worry. You just correct your path and continue to your desired destination.

You don't give up. You're not going to stop towards the end of your journey and turn back are you? You will keep going. Even if you get a little lost at the end you don't stop until you get there. Unlike the sat nav, the Universe doesn't give you an estimated time of arrival at your destination. Although, that is the only difference between this analogy and the reality of manifesting with the Law of Attraction.

Then one day, when you least expect it, you wake up and realise that you have arrived at your destination. Blessings.

"Few realize that they can control the way they feel and positively affect the things that come into their life experience by deliberately directing their thoughts."
—Abraham Hicks

Chapter 10:
Listening to Your Body

"I lovingly listen to my body's messages"

Following Your Intuition

Gut feeling, sixth sense, instinct, mother's intuition, Inner Ding or Inner Life Coach. Whatever you call it, you know the feeling I'm referring to right now. That feeling in the pit of your stomach when you just *know* something is right. Or, more commonly, as is so often the case in the beginning, that feeling in the pit of your stomach when you just *know* something is wrong. That little voice inside you. Louise Hay calls it your *Inner Ding*. Mothers tend to find that this instinct gets a lot stronger with motherhood. And when we go against it, we get an almost sick feeling inside. This is intuition and it is this feeling and communication channel you need to cultivate to guide you further down your healing path to happiness.

My first experience of feeling this was when my son had one of his vaccinations. I was feeling uneasy beforehand and wasn't getting clear answers to my concerns from the doctors, yet I let them literally *push* me into going ahead with it. As soon as the needle came out of his little body, I just knew I'd made the wrong call. Sometimes, we have to go against the grain to uphold the advice our intuition gives us. I was overwhelmed with the responsibility of being a parent at the time. It was ultimately my decision but I had allowed myself to be bullied by doctors. If I had had greater experience with this feeling, this inner guidance I was getting, maybe I could have been stronger. I let the supposed powers that be, talk me out of my concerns when I should have listened to the only one true power. The one inside me. The one inside all of us. Sometimes we think we haven't got a choice but we *always* have a choice even if the right choice ruffles feathers we are free to make it.

There was indeed a big lesson for me to learn that day. The lesson to trust my intuition. Trust this strange, and sometimes, uncomfortable feeling inside. It is there for a reason. To guide us. To help us make the right decisions. To help us live in alignment with our greatest good and for the greatest good of others.

I have already stressed the importance of raising your vibrations and I have covered many different ways in which you can achieve it. As your vibrations rise your intuition is heightened. The more you can listen to your own intuition, the better. This is the guidance you ultimately seek. This is where all your answers will and can be found.

In my opinion, one of the main purposes of meditation is to calm the body and mind enough to hear what this Inner Life Coach of ours is saying. You don't have to be lying down with your eyes closed although I would advise this when starting out. What we really want to do is put our conscious minds on the back burner for a while and let our subconscious minds take over. That is where our intuition can be more easily found. This simple breathing routine can really help. Breathe in slowly for a count of four, hold for a count of four and breathe out slowly for a count of eight. Repeat this slowly a few times and you will feel much more connected.

Have you ever noticed that creative thoughts come to you more often as you fall asleep or just as you wake up? This is why Paul McCartney, like many musicians, famously slept with a notebook and pen beside his bed. Do your best ideas come to you while you're jogging? How often do you find that things flow in your head effortlessly while driving? Or at the gym? Or while daydreaming? This is because we are relaxing our conscious minds and temporarily putting our egos to one side. We are allowing our all-powerful subconscious to come to the fore. We are opening up our channel to Source energy and that all important voice inside of us is being heard. This is where all the answers and guidance you need lie.

Have you also noticed that most of the activities mentioned above are enjoyable, healthy activities? Ones that you can be so engrossed and absorbed in that you, not only do it subconsciously, but you also enjoy losing track of time while doing it. These are the activities you need to pursue more of. Anything that comes to you from within during these times needs to be heeded and acted upon. This is when your body really speaks to you. When your conscious mind and its ego are elsewhere.

Theta healing is a modality whereby they use the theta stage of sleep to *tune into* this intuitive guidance. Theta is the sleep stage just as you fall asleep and just as you wake up. This is great as we are provided with an opportunity at least twice a day in which to tap into our intuition.

Remember we can ask our intuition questions too. When we get sick it is, in fact, our body's way of communicating with us and letting us know that something is wrong. Once in that calm, relaxed state with your conscious mind put to the side, ask your body what it is you need to know. Ask what it is that you need in order to heal. Whatever idea pops into your head will probably be the right answer. Trust it.

The really cool thing about following your intuition and, by doing so, your Divine path is that you can't go wrong. You may think you can, at the time, but you can't. And when fear rears its ugly head, as it does, and tells you that you can't do whatever it is, for whatever reason, usually money, you have to learn to release that fear. That's where *faith* comes in.

Faith

"Why not take a chance on Faith. Not religion but Faith. Not hope but Faith ... Hope walks though the fire and Faith leaps over it!"
—*Jim Carrey*

Admittedly it's hard to have faith at first. That's why we call it *Blind Faith*. However, the more you follow your intuition and, the more it serves you well, which it will, the more faith you will have. Trusting your intuition is basically, the same as having faith. You develop faith in your intuition and they grow together.

When we follow our Divine Path the Universe will see to it that we are supported. "How?" is not for us to ask, but it will. This knowing, this faith, is what will provide you with the security you seek. Not worry or fear.

"Faith and Fear—both demand you believe in something you cannot see. You choose!"
—Bob Proctor

Have faith in yourself. There are things in your life you want to change. Be that change that you are seeking.

Have faith in your *own* abilities to heal yourself.

Have faith that your affirmations will come to fruition.

Have faith that your gratitude list will get longer and longer as the Universe brings you more and more things to be grateful for.

Have faith in your ability to release your trapped emotions with EFT and The Emotion Code or other energy healing modality you are drawn to.

Have faith that you can learn to still your mind and hear the Inner Life Coach within you.

Have faith that the Universe will guide you to the right way for you to raise your vibrations.

Have faith that you can and will be supported doing what you love and that people with the same vibrations will be there for you to meet.

Have faith that you can achieve as much happiness as *you* desire.

Have faith in yourself.

Have Faith that You can Heal Yourself to Happiness.

Listening to the Angels

I got quite into Angels a few years ago after reading and listening to some of Doreen Virtue's work. She pulls Oracle Cards each Sunday and posts a clip about them on her website and on social media. They speak to me so clearly. I was so amazed by this at first but now I understand it and, having completed her online Angel Card Reading course, I pull my own cards now and the guidance is equally clear. I had a very powerful dream whereby Archangel Raphael came to me, with his shining emerald light, and told me, in no uncertain terms, that I was a healer. He told me that, not only could I heal myself and my life, but that I should also follow a path of helping others to heal themselves.

Talking to a natural healer friend of mine, who has greatly inspired me over the years, I referred to the Angels one day. She was very matter of fact in her response that Angels don't exist. She told me they were *"just a manifestation of energy"*. At first I felt quite disappointed. I had always learned a lot of *truth* from her and I really didn't want to believe that Angels didn't exist. I had learned to love them so much.

Then it dawned on me. Of course they are just a manifestation of energy! Everything is just a manifestation of energy. We are all just manifestations of energy. I am just a manifestation of energy and I believe in myself. The Angels are in the 5th (or higher) dimension and like everything else there, they are in fact, as Abraham puts it, *"a nebulous mist"*. How we view them and perceive them is up to us and I'm happy with my perception of the Angels. It works for me and the important thing, in my opinion, is listening to the messages they bring and the guidance they give.

They say when you see a white feather, butterfly, dragonfly or coin that it is an Angel watching over you. This is difficult for many to believe. The sceptics always say a white feather just means the cat has caught a bird. I ask them to think about it. Think about the thoughts they are having when they first sight that feather, butterfly or whatever. Especially if you are distracted and in your own world, in other words, when your conscious mind has been put aside for a while. If you see a sign then, think about what thoughts or idea last passed through your mind. It will be that thought or idea that has come from the Angels and it will be that thought or idea that you need to heed. It will be their guidance to you.

A few months ago, I was swimming up and down my friend's pool. Doing the thing that makes my heart sing. Thinking how wonderful my life was. Raising my vibrations. My conscious mind put aside. I was letting my mind wander. I had the sudden idea to write a book. It came to me out of the blue. Then I saw a tiny white feather in the water. It made me smile. I know the Angels are watching over me. Then I saw another. Then a white butterfly flew by and hovered over my head. I thought again about the idea I'd just had to write a book. Another butterfly came by and a dragonfly. It was a party of Angels. They were clearly telling me to write a book. So I did. Thank you for reading it.

Blessings
xx

"If you can Dream it, You can do it."

Book and Website References

You Can Heal Your Life by Louise Hay (1984) Hay House, Inc., Carlsbad, CA

The Honeymoon Effect by Dr Bruce Lipton PhD (2014), Hay House, Inc., Carlsbad, CA

The Biology of Belief by Dr Bruce Lipton PhD (2008), Hay House, Inc., Carlsbad, CA

Power Vs Force by Dr David Hawkins (2014), Hay House, Inc., Carlsbad, CA

Nurturing Healing Love by Scarlett Lewis (2014), Hay House, Inc., Carlsbad, CA

The Tapping Solution by Nick Ortner (2013), Hay House, Inc., Carlsbad, CA

The Secret by Rhonda Byrne, Atria (2006)

For further information about The Emotion Code, The Body Code, and magnets, go to www.healerslibrary.com

Masaru Emoto's Water Crystals www.masaru-emoto.net/english/water-crystal.html

PSYCH K® https://www.psych-k.com

I also recommend reading and/or watching anything by Dr Wayne Dyer, Doreen Virtue and Mike Dooley (from Hay House).

Acknowledgments

"When the student is ready the right teacher will appear"—Chinese Proverb

I'd like to thank all the teachers and Earth Angels who I've met on my journey and those who I have yet to meet. You have touched my heart. You know who you are. I'd also like to thank the dear friends who have shared the journey with me.

I'd also like to take this opportunity to thank all of my clients, past and present, who have taught me so much and have helped me grow and find the happy place in which I now find myself.

Finally, I need to seriously thank my beloved husband and son who have, quite literally, put up with me during the birth of this book. I am so very blessed to have these two wonderful men in my life.

If you have enjoyed reading this book please leave a helpful review on Amazon or get in touch and tell me what you think.

www.deborahjanesutton.com

Blessings
xx

Author Bio

Deborah Jane Sutton is an Energy Healer, Self Healing Coach and author. She is also her own best advert. In the last few years, by following the steps she outlines in her book, she has learned to love her own company, lost 20 kilos, not seen a doctor, met and married her Mr Right and has finally left the 'day job' to follow her heart.

Originally from Sussex in the UK, Deborah now lives among the orange groves of Valencia in Spain with her husband, son and various animals. She walks her talk and keeps her vibrations high by doing the things she loves— walking, swimming, yoga, writing, coaching and spending time with her family. She enjoys learning new healing modalities and philosophies so she can better serve her clients. Deborah is passionate about spreading the simplicity of self healing and sees it as her contribution to creating a better world for us all.

Deborah also runs Healing Holidays with her husband from their Villa where she helps guests Heal themselves to Happiness.

To find out more about Deborah and her work visit:

www.deborahjanesutton.com

Printed in Great Britain
by Amazon